DESIGN
FOR
STORY

DESIGN FOR STORY

CREATE IMMERSIVE OUTDOOR LIVING EXPERIENCES

NOAH NEHLICH

STRUCTURE BOOKS
LAS VEGAS · NEVADA

Design for Story:
Create Immersive Outdoor Living Experiences
Copyright © 2020 by Noah Nehlich
All rights reserved.
First Edition: 2020

ISBN: 979-8-633-53649-2 (Paperback)
ISBN: 978-0-578-67352-3 (Hard Cover)

Writer: Shannon Siggeman
Cover and Artwork: Michael Malaska

No part of this book may be reproduced, scanned, or distributed in any printed or electronic form without permission. Please do not participate in or encourage piracy of copyrighted materials in violation of the author's rights. Thank you for respecting the hard work of this author.

Although the author has made every effort to ensure that the information in this book was correct at press time, the author does not assume and hereby disclaims any liability to any party for any loss, damage, or disruption caused by errors or omissions, whether such errors or omissions result from negligence, accident, or any other cause.

For designers who strive
to create unforgettable experiences.

TABLE OF CONTENTS

PREFACE ... ix

ACKNOWLEDGMENTS ... xiii

ONE: SELL THEIR STORIES, NOT YOUR DESIGN ... 1

TWO: MAKE CONNECTIONS ... 25

THREE: YOU ARE THE EXPERT ... 49

FOUR: DESIGN IN 3D—AND IN PHASES ... 73

FIVE: SURPRISE YOUR CLIENTS ... 93

SIX: CREATE AN EXPERIENCE ... 111

SEVEN: SHARE WITH PURPOSE ... 137

APPENDIX: HOW TO CHARGE FOR YOUR DESIGNS ... 163

NOTES ... 175

BIBLIOGRAPHY ... 191

ABOUT THE AUTHOR ... 205

PREFACE

QUITE A FEW TECH COMPANY origin stories begin in some atypical offices: Bill Gates and Paul Allen started Microsoft in a famously small Albuquerque garage. Steve Jobs, Steve Wozniak, and Ronald Wayne started what would become Apple in a Los Altos garage. Facebook began in Mark Zuckerberg's Harvard dorm. And Google was started by Larry Page and Sergey Brin in Susan Wojcicki's garage in Menlo Park.

Just a year after Google was founded, Structure Studios, too, would get its start in equally unofficial quarters: my childhood bedroom. It was there in that bedroom—slouching in an old chair rather more than current ergonomic wisdom would advise, working on a desktop computer I'd cobbled together—that I realized the 3D program I had been tinkering with was more than just a distraction from other homework I'd been putting off.

That first program transformed me from a student into an entrepreneur. It was also about to transform the pool industry: that software—soon known as Pool Studio, and later to be joined by VizTerra, Vip3D, and YARD—was what made 3D design accessible to everyone. You didn't need deep corporate pockets, and you didn't need to dedicate years to a computer science degree. All you needed was a straightforward gaming computer—the same kind, with the same hardware specs, that you could pick up just about anywhere—and you could use our software to show your clients incredible 3D pools that were like nothing they'd ever seen before. You could create an experience.

Starting out in that unofficial office as we did, I figured we were in pretty good company. If Google could make the Internet accessible to everyone, then we could make 3D design accessible to everyone, too.

At the time, however, I didn't exactly look the part of a pool guy—or, at least, not like a guy who spent much time lounging around pools. When my team and I started developing the software that would become Pool Studio, I was a former student about as pale as the paper this book is printed on, digging for loose change to afford a taco for lunch. The pool industry welcomed me anyway.

And since my first meeting with one of the giants of the industry—Paramount's Buzz Ghiz—I've continued to meet many incredibly thoughtful and phenomenally creative people who share my belief that 3D is much more than just a neat tool. Improving lives through 3D experiences is our goal, and to achieve that goal, we focus on much more than just the code that forms the basis of our products.

People, after all, aren't building pools to have something to look at from their kitchen windows. And they're not installing landscaping merely to give the neighborhood kid who mows their lawn something to navigate the mower around. What they want, instead, is to enjoy the backyard of their dreams: the fun or sophisticated or even surprising space where their kids will play, their friends will hang out, and their guests will feel welcome.

Helping pool and landscape designers create exciting, immersive experiences for their clients is what motivated us as we set out to develop the best 3D design software. Nearly twenty years later, that first 3D program has grown to reach users far beyond the walls of my childhood bedroom. Worldwide, designers, builders, landscape architects, and more create beautiful designs and presentations that are far more realistic and interactive than most of their clients ever imagine would be possible, complete with professional-quality videos, photo-realistic screenshots, 360-degree images explorable from any angle, and even sound effects that range from kids splashing in the pool to birds chirping in the shade trees.

We've even taken presentations beyond 3D, first with virtual reality and then with the first augmented-reality app developed for outdoor living designers: YARD. To get there, we asked two simple questions:

What does it really take to sell a pool?

And how could we make that process a little bit easier on everyone?

To answer those questions, we turned to the same people who would amaze us with the incredible designs they'd quickly begin to create: our Members. From the very beginning, our software users have shared their opinions and experiences with us. We love that, because that is how we figure out what's working, what's not, and what we need to get to work developing, *fast*. That also means we get to hear some pretty amazing stories just about every day. Listed on their own, the numbers almost defy belief:

- Jim has achieved a 75% closing ratio.
- A mere four years after Craig started out mowing lawns, he started designing six-figure pools for million-dollar properties.
- The first day Tom used Pool Studio, he designed a $42,000 pool right at his client's kitchen table—and got the contract signed minutes later.

In a television commercial, those numbers would come with a disclaimer voiced as quickly as by an auctioneer: *results not typical*. And yet, for nearly twenty years now, stories like these have just kept coming in. We've learned a lot from the designers and builders who've shared their stories with us—and we, in turn, are now sharing what we've learned from those stories.

As Benjamin Franklin wrote:

> *"Either write things worth reading,
> or do things worth the writing."*[1]

We've met quite a few overachieving designers, builders, and landscape architects who manage to do both. The stories they've shared are more than worth the writing because we think their insights are absolutely worth reading.

What they share in common is not just their appreciation of 3D design software but also their ability to tell a great story. That ability—plus their well-honed listening skills—is what truly sets them apart. After all, who wants to play even the most visually exciting video game without a story driving the action? Who cares how beautiful a movie is when the characters are boring?

The amazing designs, stories, and presentations that designers have created for their clients—and shared with us—are in many ways exactly like a great movie or an engaging novel or a compelling video game. Maybe what it takes to sell a pool or a landscape, after all, is this: Forget the tech specs and the sales tricks. Forget about the acronyms, the stats, and even your competitors. Instead: design a story, and invite your clients to jump in and explore every detail.

—Noah Nehlich, March 2020

ACKNOWLEDGMENTS

It turns out, you can log a fair amount of time reading on airplanes when you get to travel as much as I have over the years. When I set out to answer the two big questions that have motivated us here at Structure Studios from the very beginning—"what does it take to sell a pool?" and "how can we help?"—I started by researching the latest and greatest, the best and brightest, and the tried-and-true while traveling to meetings and trade shows. It didn't take long for me to realize that the best tips and most inspirational ideas often were not the ones most loudly proclaimed as such but, instead, were the ones found where least expected.

That kid who couldn't find enough change for a taco has gotten to do and see some pretty cool stuff—and I put developing awesome 3D design software and releasing the first AR app for outdoor living designers at the top of that list. I've also gotten to see things that have encouraged me to put my love of the outdoors into a much broader context. What I learned watching a hockey game destined for the record books has been as inspirational as what I saw when I got the chance to stand in front of the 600-year-old dome that makes the skyline of Florence so distinctive. Sometimes, the title of an article alone was enough to spark some pretty fascinating conversations. Other times, checking an item off my bucket list encouraged me to see challenges in new ways—and helped me appreciate the value of a research study in ways I would not have expected.

After all, many of the challenges that designers face today are the same ones that Renaissance artists, nineteenth-century novelists, and twentieth-century filmmakers faced when not just trying to create something spectacular, but also when trying to help their clients (or their audiences) understand why what they were creating was so valuable.

There's a story behind every design, I learned, and this book is the result of that realization. Those books, articles, and studies that I read were just the start. The ideas and stories in this book have also been informed by the conversations I've had and the friendships I've made with the many excellent designers, builders, sales guys, and others who have made me feel so welcome in the industry—and also with the ones whom I, in turn, have been able to welcome.

Buzz Ghiz, Bill Burt, and Joe Vassallo were the first to make me feel at home in the industry; their thoughtful advice and continued encouragement have been invaluable to me for many years. I would like to thank, too, Barry Justus, Damon Lang, Jeromey Naugle, Jim Bellamy, John Kay, John Ogburn, Lea Frederick, Shane LeBlanc, and Tod Brown for generously and graciously contributing their stories and insights. I am also grateful to the numerous others who have shared their funny, touching stories of the occasional mishaps and miscommunications that can occur in this business; some of those stories have been anonymized.

I would also like to thank Shannon Siggeman, who helped me tell the story I wanted to share with you; Stefanie Dunn, whose organizational expertise made this book a joy to complete; Michael Malaska, whose illustrations brought to life many of the ideas in this book; Patrick Smith, who joined me at the very beginning and dedicated his unmatched engineering talent to fulfilling our shared goal of improving lives through 3D design; and the entire world-class team at Structure Studios. We're a team that loves the outdoors as much as we love developing software; our love for the first drives our love for the second, spurring us on as we achieve our goal of improving lives through exceptional 3D experiences.

DESIGN
FOR
STORY

ONE

SELL THEIR STORIES, NOT YOUR DESIGN

*A whole is that which has a beginning,
a middle, and an end.*
—Aristotle[2]

For seven years, Sean O'Neil[3] didn't see the point in changing how he showed his pool designs to his clients. Every year, he attended a trade show or two to check out the latest technology, but no matter how many times he returned to see the 3D presentations, he never felt the need to start designing in 3D—why, he figured, change what was already working so well?

It didn't seem like a big deal to him, anyway: a 3D pool just looked like a pool, and he had seen thousands of pools. He noticed the software seemed easy enough to use, so he decided to give it a try. When he was putting together plans for his next client's backyard renovation, he drew a quick pool in 3D and added it to his design before he headed over to their meeting. To his surprise, as he began to reveal the pool he had designed in 3D, his client started to cry. Startled by her reaction, Sean asked, "What's wrong? What's wrong with it?"

She said, "It's been my dream my whole life to have a swimming pool. And now it's real! It's here. There it is! That's my dream!"

Transforming a homeowner's mundane backyard into a

dream retreat is what many pool designers promise to do for their clients. On websites and social media accounts, even on flyers and mailers, that promise is spelled out: *we'll build you the backyard of your dreams.*

Sometimes, however, even when you know that the design you are offering your client is exactly right for their family, it can be hard to help them fully understand its merits. Over the years, we've talked to many designers who have struggled to get an indecisive client to choose—and many more who are looking for ways to help make it a little bit easier for clients to make that decision to build. Designers, builders, landscape architects, and more, from warm and sunny climates as well as cold and snowy ones around the world, are looking for answers to the same questions: What, ultimately, is it that motivates a client to sign on the spot? What makes them hesitate, and what inspires them to say, "There it is! That's my dream!" What makes a client feel that they are looking at *their* pool?

The answers sometimes seem self-evident: maybe the design really is that great. Maybe the designer's years of experience building the exact style of pool that the client wants helped them hit it out of the park. However, as Sean saw when he offered his client that personalized 3D pool design, the happiest clients are the ones who don't just see a beautiful design by a great designer. Instead, the happiest clients are those who choose a design not only because it is beautiful and not only because the designer is skilled but also because the design is giving them something extra: a personalized experience that reassures them that the design is exactly right for their family.

364 Million Ways to Tell a Story

A great story—not just a pretty good one or a pretty interesting one, but a genuinely great one that inspires listeners to shed tears of joy—is often thought of as either the result of a fortuitous knack for spinning a yarn…or of copious amounts of blood, sweat, and tears. Perhaps it's only in movies that a plucky underdog—or a mysterious Keyser Söze—can reel in listeners with stories concocted on the fly.

Even artists as indisputably talented as Michelangelo have questioned their ability to talk about the art they have created. Michelangelo himself—who, in addition to being a painter and sculptor, was also a poet—was not especially fond of the writing process: "writing," he admitted in a letter, "is a great affliction to me, for it is not my art."[4]

According to his biographer, Giorgio Vasari, Michelangelo's lack of confidence in his writing ability prevented him from sharing all of his ideas: "[Michelangelo] told me several times, in spite of his age he would often have made anatomical studies, and would have written upon them, for the benefit of his fellow-craftsmen… But he did not trust himself, through not being able to express himself in writing as he would have liked."[5]

Michelangelo is not the only artist to view writing as a hardship. So entrenched is the belief that the creative process is a challenging one that not only do many movies and novels frequently depict artists as struggling and scriveners as penniless, but also more than one horror movie has set a blocked and frustrated writer in a decidedly remote location. Against such ready examples, the steady routine of a prolific and successful author like Stephen King might start to seem less probable than the more chaotic process of, say, *Little Women*'s Jo March, who not only had a "scribbling suit" to wear when inspiration struck but whose family also took note of the state of that ink-stained suit when deciding whether to approach the author—who was regularly "seized" with "despair."[6] Even more familiar an example might be that of Tennessee Williams. Years before he completed one of his most well-known works, *A Streetcar Named*

Desire, Williams is said to have fueled his late nights writing with black coffee after working long days as a clerk.

If planning even an already familiar story—like the anatomical studies Michelangelo considered writing about—can seem like an inevitably time-consuming ordeal, then telling a great one without the long hours, ink stains, or black coffee might seem like an improbable feat.

In 1997, Robert McKee offered one answer to the question of how to write a compelling story when he published the storytelling strategies that have inspired Hollywood screenwriters ever since. More than twenty years later, his book, *Story*, is still widely considered the gold standard.[7]

Even the very best screenwriting or storytelling tips, however, are still just the start of the story, as it were. No matter how exceptional the design or expertly devised the presentation, a homeowner still needs to make a choice. How to help any given client make that choice is the subject of considerable research. And, as even a cursory glance through business journals full of sales tips and marketing advice will reveal, the traditional sales funnel alone is no longer the default option when helping a client make a purchasing decision.

A typical representation of a sales funnel, for example, might depict the customer as following a neat and orderly path, one that begins when they become interested in purchasing a product. Perhaps they want to barbecue in their new home's backyard, but they have only the small grill that was left behind by the previous owners. According to the traditional sales funnel, these barbecue-craving homeowners might begin by doing a little research on grills and then narrowing down their options before making a decision—orderly ushered along, of course, by a helpful salesperson.

Of course, unlike a real funnel, which would fail to serve its purpose should it unexpectedly lose any of its contents, a sales funnel typically loses quite a few prospects along the way to the final purchasing decision. Sometimes, sales tips can make it seem as though that funnel is nothing more than a numbers game—one you win simply by reaching as many prospects as possible.

Today, however, many customers—casual hot dog grillers and devoted barbecue aficionados alike—rely less on traditional advertisements and more on their own online research as well as recommendations from friends. No matter how persuasive an ad or beautiful a website, neither the text nor the visuals stand alone. The goal, therefore, is no longer to simply get in front of as many prospects as possible. It's to get those prospects actively engaged.

One way to do this: create engaging, personalized stories.

Search online for "how to tell a story," however, and you'll get 364,000,000 results in 0.60 seconds. Found within those millions of results are some tried-and-true methods for telling a compelling and meaningful story.

Turning Commodities into Must-Haves: Telling Stories that Work

What it means to tell a good story, of course, depends on your goal. Scheherazade, the famous storyteller of the classic *One Thousand and One Nights*, told her stories over the course of those 1,001 nights to pique the king's interest—and therefore to encourage him to spare her life for another night, so she could finish the story she had begun.

Kids telling scary stories to frighten each other at campfires, parents telling bedtime stories to soothe children into sleep…and salespeople trying a new approach to boosting sales numbers all rely on similar strategies to hold their listener's interest. Studying these formal strategies, however, can feel as appealing as returning to a high school Composition 101 class, where (seemingly) rigid requirements demand the thesis, the supporting evidence, and the conclusion all fall neatly into place.

Even Robert McKee's much-loved, best-selling book is not the final answer on how to tell a story. Many others have shared their own books full of tips for aspiring storytellers as well. A team of screenwriters, Robert Ben Garant and Thomas Lennon, have even published a book—*Writing Movies for Fun and Profit: How We Made a Billion Dollars at the Box Office and You Can, Too!*—that stands in humorous contrast to McKee's. As their title suggests, their book is intended less for writers seeking to understand the formal process of structuring exquisitely crafted stories and more for curious readers who want to know how the authors created the stories that earned them so much money at the box office.

For designers who want to sell more projects, the best path is found somewhere in between. Digging through those 364,000,000 online search results, you might find a fair number of useful tips on how to tell a story. In fact, you might also notice that quite a few of the early advertising gurus (including familiar names like David Ogilvy and slightly less familiar ones, too, like Claude Hopkins) continue to be featured and highlighted in many articles and lists. They remain relevant today in large part because the stories they told were so compelling that they could transform previously unknown products (like orange juice) into nearly indispensable fixtures of modern life.

Strategy #1: Be the First to Tell the Story

When Sean found himself surprised by his client's reaction to his 3D design, the reason for his surprise was simple: he didn't see precisely the same thing that she saw. To Sean, that pool was still just a plan in the works: "She started crying because it was 'real'," he points out, "but it was not a real pool yet! I had just designed it in a couple of minutes." Sean was also very aware of exactly how much work it would take to make it real: "It wasn't paid for yet, so we hadn't even scheduled it, let alone started to build it!"

To his client, however, that 3D presentation offered far more than she had imagined would be possible. For the very first time, she could see herself genuinely enjoying her new backyard with her family, because she could picture herself inside the story that had been created for her. That 3D pool was *her* pool, and, as far as she was concerned, it was as good as in her yard.

By combining the story of her future pool with his design, Sean didn't have to do much extra work to help her see what was possible: he simply used his design as the basis of an incredible story for his client. He did not merely offer his client an image of a beautiful pool. Instead, he incorporated the details of his design into his interactive presentation, helping her see how he would build the pool and yard of her dreams. The 3D pool helped him bring that story to life.

The strategy Sean used is an especially effective way to help clients see the merits of options that might not seem notably different at first glance. What made Sean's pool design different from all of the others his client had previously been offered was that Sean took the time to build the story of her yard around her beautiful new pool. In so doing, he followed a strategy that legendary advertiser Claude Hopkins identified as remarkably successful nearly one hundred years before Sean designed that pool: he told a better story, first.

Hopkins' analysis of why it is so important to tell a better story reveals an important step that can be easily overlooked (perhaps because it seems so obvious): identifying the specific details that will intrigue clients.[8] In examining the success of the approach he developed to advertise beer, Hopkins revealed why identifying relevant details is so important.

Much like those flyers and websites that promise to deliver the pool and landscape of the homeowner's dreams, the beer brewers that Hopkins analyzed all promised to deliver "pure" beer. And, as Hopkins learned, the beer brewing process was one that did not vary much: the story of how beer was brewed, after all, was not a new one. To brewers, that process was as familiar as designing pools was to Sean O'Neil. To beer drinkers, however, the highly specific details of how beer was brewed and purified, as described and illustrated in Hopkins' advertising campaign, were as fascinating as Sean's pool was to his delighted client.

By incorporating a vivid 3D design into his usual presentation process, Sean followed a strategy that Hopkins might have readily recognized: he stretched beyond his typical presentation method in order to include vivid details that were not just new and delightful to his client, they were also easy to follow and understand. Equally important: he was the first to offer his client an interactive view of what her yard could become. That strategy works because, when the client's story is aligned with the design, telling the story of the design—or the beer-making process—is the best way to tell the most compelling story.

Strategy #2: Test Your Stories (with Data!)

To analyze the success of his advertising campaigns, Claude Hopkins and his team tallied their results by hand, using the information they gathered to immediately modify and improve their approach.[9] For more than a century, tests like Hopkins' have been used to measure how successful (or effective, or persuasive) one variable is compared to another. The variable being tested might be as simple as a button on a website: do people click on a green or blue button more frequently?

Today, the results of such tests are typically measured automatically. Marketers will run an A/B test to determine whether, for example, the green or blue button performs better. Others might turn to multivariate statistics in order to assess multiple variables at once. However, for designers—especially designers who earn clients through word-of-mouth recommendations rather than from advertising—deciding what is worth tracking and measuring might not be immediately apparent.

The success of Sean's pool presentation and Hopkins' beer campaign alike suggest that such testing does not need to be undertaken on a large scale to determine what makes an approach worthwhile. Testing a process or an approach or a story to determine which version is more successful doesn't require a statistician or even an IT specialist. Testing—both when Hopkins and his team meticulously analyzed by hand the campaign results and when Sean decided to take the plunge and give the technology he'd encountered at trade shows a try—is a continuous process, one that offers benefits whether using a software program to rigorously analyze variables or conducting a quick postmortem after a project has been completed.

Perfecting stories by testing them was how Hopkins achieved some of his most notable successes—and the results of some of those successes remain notable today. For example, that rigorous approach was how Hopkins transformed oranges from a fruit eaten only occasionally into a staple of American breakfasts. In fact, since Hopkins shared the story of how healthy orange juice was in 1916, the beverage has remained popular. One hundred years later, the citrus industry has grown considerably, with the USDA reporting nearly 48 million metric tons of oranges produced worldwide.[10] In Florida alone, nearly 90% of harvested fruit is turned into juice.[11]

Hopkins rigorously tested and refined every story he told, determining along the way which stories to avoid and which to continue telling, and using the data collected to make sure that he was sharing the most compelling story with his audience. (A process that also made him an impressive amount of money.)

And he attributed his success to the care he took in planning and refining those stories. He, like Sean O'Neil, wasn't afraid to experiment and test changes. As both demonstrate, sometimes trying out a new approach is the best way to achieve better results—especially when the original approach seems to have been working just fine. Simple oranges became much-loved orange juice, just as Sean's design earned a reaction far more positive than any of his sketches had garnered in the past.

Building a compelling story at the same time as you design your client's new outdoor living space is a skill—and it's one worth mastering if you want to engage your clients with your design.

How to Tell a Story

Consider three well-known sayings:

- Tell, don't sell.
- Show, don't tell.
- A picture is worth 1,000 words.

Pithy as they may be, they don't exactly offer much in the way of practical advice. What, you might ask, really is the distinction between telling and selling or showing and telling? As any kindergartner excited for Show-and-Tell knows, the two go hand in hand: it's the day in school when kids get to bring their favorite things to class to share with their fellow students.

If you talk to many pool and landscape designers, you might find that some occasionally feel as though the day in, day out routine can become a little bit too mundane. On days like those, they might feel like they are just heading to yet another client's house to show yet another design and then figure out some way to get the client to say yes. Then it's just a matter of getting the contract signed before they head to the next lead. Maybe this time it's a pool and some pavers; maybe next time it'll be an outdoor kitchen and landscaping.

When the showing and the telling feel mundane, it can start to feel like you're really just there to sell concrete or rocks or trees or water. That's certainly not quite as exciting a prospect as Show-and-Tell is for your kids.

Instead try creating a better experience and telling a better story—an engaging, compelling, interactive one that is your client's own. If you return to those 364,000,000 search results on "how to tell a story" for advice, you will likely come across some common narrative structures:

- Three parts: Greek philosopher Aristotle suggested that an ideal structure would include three parts. "A whole is that which has a beginning, a middle, and an end."[12]
- Four parts: Chinese, Korean, and Japanese stories often follow a structure known as Kishōtenketsu, which includes four parts: the introduction, development, unexpected twist, and conclusion.
- Five parts: Nineteenth-century German writer Gustav Freytag added more detail to Aristotle's structure when he developed a five-part template that would become known as "Freytag's Pyramid."

You might follow Aristotle or Freytag to plot a play or novel. You might use the Kishōtenketsu structure to develop a video game story. However, for a designer—especially one who doesn't want to get bogged down or sidetracked by Composition 101 narrative theory—applying the best storytelling techniques to a design presentation is not a matter of strictly following prescribed rules. What inspires clients to buy a pool isn't the tech specs of the pool or the decking, and it isn't the list of shrubs you will plant in their yard. It very likely isn't your Shakespearean dedication to iambic pentameter or your Aristotelian devotion to the rules of drama, either.

The rules, after all, are meant to help make the story better. A strictly structured presentation isn't any more likely to sway a client than cold, hard statistics about concrete yardage or rebar spacing would. If all of the elements of the story don't work together, then merely ticking off requirements on a "How to Tell a Story" checklist won't be enough.

When Aristotle compared the process of telling a story to painting a portrait, he noted that "The most beautiful [colors], laid on confusedly, will not give as much pleasure as the chalk outline of a portrait."[13] What matters is not the mere fact that the "colors"—or, say, the features of the design—are beautiful. If the features are too complicated and confusing for a client to understand, then it won't matter how beautiful they might be. A simple, recognizable chalk outline, Aristotle suggests, would be more enjoyable than a beautiful painting the viewer can't understand.

Creating a great story entails figuring out how to tell your client their own meaningful story—one that they will clearly recognize as their own. It's about getting them to see how your story—your design—gives them what they really want and makes their lives better. And no matter how many moving parts that story has, two main elements are fundamental to our enjoyment of a story: the characters and the plot.

So fundamental to a good story are the characters and the plot that, if you were to ask someone to tell you about their favorite movie or novel, both elements would likely be inextricably intertwined in their retelling. "It's about this guy," they might begin, "and he has to…." Maybe he has to solve a mystery. Maybe she has to fight off an alien. During awards ceremonies, the nominations that spark the most excitement aren't the technical ones, no matter how impressive the technical feats achieved in the service of solving that mystery or fighting off that alien may have been. What viewers eagerly discuss and debate, instead, is which actor gave the best performance, or which director made the best movie.

Dedicated fans might analyze the intricacies of a movie's plot, eagle-eyed viewers might search for "Easter eggs" (and bloopers), and curious artists might admire the innovative techniques put to use. However, the top movies that have earned the most money at the worldwide box office do not earn their rankings through those feats alone. It's the characters—and the adventures they undergo—that capture the imagination.

Characters: Is a Picture Really Worth 1,000 Words?

The first thing any good story needs? Characters.

Before a character can be brought to life in a movie or a novel or a presentation, that character needs to be developed. During the character development process, a storyteller will often identify and decide upon far more traits or habits or details than they will include in their finished story. Great stories, however, don't need to include an overabundance of detail to connect with their audience: a picture, not 1,000 extra words of exposition, will suffice.

For example, viewers did not need to know much about John McClane for his character to resonate immediately. They did not need to know that the movie he first appeared in was based on a novel written by Roderick Thorp, *Nothing Lasts Forever*, and they certainly did not need to have read that book to enjoy the movie. McClane wasn't a superhero; he was an everyday guy, just trying to do his job and get through his day. That guy appealed so much to viewers that *Die Hard* became a billion-dollar franchise.

To create an appealing story featuring your clients enjoying their new outdoor living space, you don't need to write a novel to examine every single imaginable detail about them. What you need, instead, is to ask the questions that will help you build a picture that reveals your characters.

Discover Your Characters:

When you arrive at a client's home, ready to figure out the characters for the story you're about to create, you might begin with the five (or even six) classic questions that writers (and students, journalists, business consultants, and even project managers) regularly use to narrow their focus: who, what, where, when, why, and the bonus sixth question, how.

Your client's answers to those questions help you shape their unique, personalized story. A great pool and landscape designer, after all, doesn't just churn out cookie-cutter pools for cookie-cutter clients, one right after the other. A great designer approaches a new customer's house the same way that Hopkins walked into that beer company: ready to discover what makes that client unique.

- Who are your clients, *really*?
- What do they like and what do they want to change about their outdoor living space?
- Where are the trouble areas in their outdoor living space?
- When do they—and when do they *not*—enjoy spending time in their yard?
- Why is their current space not working for them?
- How do they want to use their outdoor living space—and how can you help?

Starting with basic questions like these helps you gather the information you need to ask even more thoughtful questions about how your clients would like to use and enjoy their outdoor living space:

- Do they have kids, and maybe a dog? If so, do they want a yard where all the neighborhood kids will come to play? Or do they want a private place where their kids (and the family dog) can play safely?
- Do they throw parties? How often? How many people do they invite? Do they like to throw daytime pool parties or evening dinner parties?
- Do they want a retreat where they can escape from the stress of work and the real world?
- What do they enjoy about their home? How is their home decorated, and how did they choose that style? If a prominent art piece or decoration is on display, how did they choose it and where is it from?
- Do they want an outdoor living space that they can view and enjoy from inside their house?

That last question—do they want to enjoy their yard from inside the house, too—is one that many homeowners overlook in their enthusiasm for renovating their outdoor living space. However, many pools and landscapes are actually enjoyed just as much when viewed from inside the house as when the family is outdoors—especially during the winter months. Making sure the view is enjoyable from the indoors is an extra detail that's easy to add to a design—and it's the type of detail that helps reveal why your custom design is exactly right for your clients.

Set the Stage for Your Characters:

If you are not meeting with the homeowner directly, taking the time to answer detailed questions about who your clients might be is a beneficial strategy that will help you shape your design story. If, for example, you are meeting with an architect who is building a house on spec, it's likely that that architect already has an ideal homebuyer in mind. What is that client like? Is the home intended for a family with kids or a retired couple? Is it for athletes interested in fitness, a chef interested in organic gardening, or an executive hosting parties for clients?

When you do not yet know who the characters inhabiting your design story will be, answering questions about who they might be helps you to set the stage for them. In fact, that strategy is often used by real estate agents when staging homes.

In real estate, staged spaces work not by offering a cookie-cutter version of "luxury" but instead by identifying the characters of the story they are staging: who are the next owners going to be, what will they want, and how can we give them what they want?

In cities, for example, even high-end luxury apartments are often so small in size that special features can be easily overwhelmed by the current owner's belongings. When a living space might be compared to a shoebox, and when that shoebox might seem like it is already crammed full of someone else's stuff, then it can be challenging for a realtor to help their clients imagine themselves living the aspirational lifestyle they want in that crowded shoebox of a space.

However, simply cleaning up the place, removing anything too personal, and popping some cookie dough in the oven is rarely, if ever, the winning strategy. Far from eliminating all signs of personality, many real estate agents and stagers instead choose to add and highlight carefully selected elements—including artwork, furniture, and accessories—to create a picture or tell a story that will help buyers imagine themselves living the life they want in that space.

Taking the time to imagine who the future homeowners will be and what they might enjoy, whether indoors or outdoors, helps sets the stage for the next important step in telling your client's unique story: developing the plot.

Plot: Enter the Family Dog

If staging a property is one of the most popular ways realtors create a sense of connection to a home for sale, then populating a design with to-scale human figures—which architects refer to as "scalies"—is one important way designers help clients not just connect with plans but also understand the scale of them.

When realtors stage a space with carefully chosen furniture, artwork, and accessories, they do so in order to create a sense of connection for buyers touring a home for sale. Those objects do more than simply help potential homeowners understand exactly how much space the home offers. Staging a space helps potential buyers imagine themselves living in that home with those items. If, for example, the realtor knows that the family has been looking for a house where they can host big dinner parties as well as invite all of their kids' friends over, then maybe they'll take them to tour a house staged to show that the dining room fits a table that seats ten and the family room is spacious enough to include a large table for board games as well as a comfortable sectional for movie nights. Those details might help their client decide that the house is right for them.

When the space the homeowners are considering has not yet been built, however, and when the client can't yet physically sit on the chairs or gaze out the windows, then it is much harder for them to understand the scale and purpose of what they are choosing. One way to help them understand the actual scale of the project is to add both 3D objects and human figures—those 3D "scalies"—to your interactive presentation, revealing how your design suits their space and their lifestyle as you lead them through the plot of the design's story.

People aren't the only figures worth adding to a design. One of the most popular 3D objects to share in a presentation, in fact, is the family dog.[14] Whether napping in the sun on the deck or wading in the pool, the family dog is more than just another way to help the client understand the scale of a design. Including the dog is a meaningful way to connect a homeowner to your design emotionally as well as visually. (Had Sean added his client's dog to the 3D pool he'd created for her, she, like many of the other clients for whom Sean would soon begin to design 3D projects, might have happily exclaimed not just, "That's my pool!" but also "That's my dog!")

That process of engaging a client's emotions begins with figuring out what it is that they want. Setting your clients as the characters of your story means taking their answers to the "Discover Your Characters" questions above—How do they want to use their outdoor living space? Do they have kids? Do they like to host parties?—and building a story in response.

Once you have gathered that information, you can begin to answer the questions that will help you form the plot of your client's story:

1. What do your characters want?

This question is often the easiest to answer. What do your clients want? An outdoor living space that they can enjoy with their friends and family. Perhaps they want a pool ideal for swimming laps. Maybe they're barbecue aficionados who've decided that they also want a full outdoor kitchen to go along with their pool. If you imagine each member of the family (and each pet) as a character in your story, then your plot answers how each one will enjoy the backyard that you're designing.

2. Why don't they have it?

Many of the improvements that a homeowner might be interested in making to their outdoor living space are far from easy

DIY projects, since many of the additions a family might want to make to their yard are not ones that can quickly be finished in a few spare weekend hours. Adding a swimming pool, building a deck, or planning an outdoor kitchen: undertaking even just one of these can be a daunting task, especially when contending with challenges like an oddly shaped yard or difficult terrain. Helping your client see how your design achieves their goals and offers them what they want is an important part of your plot.

3. How can they get it?

When Hopkins analyzed his campaigns, he noticed that people prefer rewards—the carrot, as it were, to the stick.[15] Sometimes, however, salespeople rely on scare tactics—that figurative stick—to attempt to motivate clients.

Robert, a landscape architect, saw just how quickly that method could backfire when a rather nervous client kept getting sidetracked during their meeting. As he continued to ask questions, Robert learned that they had recently been visited by a gutter cleaning company. That company's salesperson had resorted to a rather clumsy take on crime-film dialogue to scare the elderly homeowner into signing a contract: "Nice house you've got," the salesperson had said, apparently one gesture away from twirling his mustache. "It would be a shame if someone slipped and fell."

There is no Shakespearean "Exit, pursued by a bear"[16] to instantly dispatch a bad guy, however, once brought into existence. Robert suspected that the gutter salesperson had probably intended to demonstrate that he had identified a problem that he could solve: he could clean their gutters to make sure rainwater drained safely away instead of settling into dangerous icy patches. His approach, however, left the client anxious instead of reassured. Instead of focusing on building a strong, trusting relationship, that salesperson had tried to scare the homeowner into compliance.

A better route: build your plot to show your clients what they'll enjoy in their new outdoor living space. Show them how you've improved their space and made their lives better. Each character included and each new element added can feature in a chapter of your story to connect your clients to your custom design.

Robert reassured his anxious homeowner by demonstrating to them how the useful safety features that he had included—like sturdy handrails and paving stones that would not be slippery in the rain—would work for everyone in their family (including their beloved arthritic Great Dane).

Start Your Next Client's Story

Creating for your clients a personalized story with captivating characters and a compelling plot begins by answering the questions that will help you establish exactly who your characters are and what they want to achieve.

Imagine a hypothetical family with two young kids and a new dog. They like to host big parties, and they frequently invite their extended family as well as their friends and neighbors to visit. What chapters will help tell their story?

1. What does this family want?

The parents have said they want a pool, an outdoor kitchen, and a deck so that they can host their frequent guests more comfortably.

2. Why don't they have it?

The family has a pretty big yard, so it seems like it would be easy to fit everything in. However, they don't know where to start or how to make everything they want "flow" together. They have a big family, so they want to be able to host big parties, but the slope of their yard has prevented them from inviting over as many people as they'd like: simply placing enough outdoor furniture for comfortable seating has been challenging. They also want a pool, but because their kids are young, they're worried about pool safety.

3. How will you help them get it?

Before you start your custom design, you might assess what you noticed during your meeting with the family to get a feel for what can and cannot be changed. You might break up their yard into zones (or chapters of your story). You might address their steeply sloped yard, for example, by giving them a multilevel deck designed with smaller zones for relaxing, cooking, and dining. You might add a pool cover as well as a secure fence so that they'll feel confident their kids will be safe.

Easy as it might be to imagine exactly how you'd put together a design for such a family, many homeowners need help understanding what makes a design really work. It's when you tell this family the story of your custom design that you help them understand exactly why your design is the one that offers them exactly what they've been looking for—and why, therefore, it's the best one for them (as well as their kids, their dog, and their big extended family).

Detailing the raw materials that go into that deck or outdoor kitchen is far less engaging for a client than explaining the story behind these features:

Parties: Earn your client's enthusiasm by highlighting features of the design that improve the flow of the space to make hosting easier. For example, you might explain that the custom pergola on the deck has been situated to help them stay cool while they watch the kids swim in the pool. The curved seating area does not just provide extra seating; it also invites guests to relax while chatting with the chef in the outdoor kitchen. And the entire deck centers on the indoor kitchen so that it is easy for the hosts to bring supplies out for the party while also offering great views of the outdoors from the interior windows.

Pets: Give any family pets their own space within the design. Their dog, for example, might enjoy a dog run or a Baja shelf in the pool to cool off in the summer. Even if their dog never uses that step in the pool, your client will feel special that you took into account everyone in their family—including the beloved family pet.

Personality: When learning more about this young family, you might notice that they're not just a friendly couple with a couple of cute kids. They also have a quirky sense of humor or a decided sense of style. People want their home to feel like their own, so being attentive to those details is an excellent way to add thoughtful touches that will make them feel like your design truly suits their family.

Key Takeaways

The most beautiful design that gives your client everything that they've asked for will seem like nothing more than an impersonal pretty picture if your client can't imagine their family actually enjoying the space you've designed.

When you present your next design, try a time-tested, research-backed, and surprisingly underused strategy: **tell your clients a story as you reveal your design.**

- What do your clients want?
- Why don't they have it?
- How are you going to help them get it?

Demonstrate your expertise and engage your client's interest by casting the family as the characters, staging your design the way a realtor might stage a house, and then revealing in your story how your design offers something for everyone (including the family dog!).

TWO

MAKE CONNECTIONS

Character is plot,
plot is character.
—Attributed to F. Scott Fitzgerald

Before Mark Zuckerberg created Facebook—and long before anyone might have imagined that Facebook would one day grow to reach more than two billion (occasionally disgruntled) users—he built a program as a college sophomore that was a bit smaller in scope. Called CourseMatch, Zuckerberg's project is said to have been intended to help students pick classes based on who else was already enrolled, an option that seemed to become popular with his fellow students immediately.

Although Facebook today has long since expanded beyond its early roots helping university students connect with one another, it retains more than a hint of CourseMatch's early promise. Whether it's college kids wanting to be sure that they are taking the right classes or it's colleagues wanting to compare who had the better weekend, many people who use social media networks like Facebook do so not only to share information about themselves but also to take a peek at just how they stack up compared to everyone else.

That very human interest in both sharing as well as comparing is why, sometimes, social media networks can serve to strengthen a client's connection to your design. In fact, sometimes the connections fostered by social media are so strong, they help homeowners sell themselves on their own future outdoor living projects.

The Self-Selling Swimming Pool

For years, Texas pool builder Paul did not think social media was particularly relevant to his business. If asked, he might have grudgingly acknowledged that social media was one way his family would catch up on what distant relatives had been up to—the modern equivalent of the vacation slideshows that his parents' generation dutifully sat through at parties. He didn't use social media much himself, and, as a busy builder who designed a few pools in the mid-to-high range every year, Paul didn't really see any reason to take the time to include it in his design or sales process.

That began to change, however, after Paul designed a custom swimming pool and complete outdoor living space for a young couple, Jason and Jennifer, who had given him a fairly extensive wish list—and a $120,000 budget. Paul had learned that they didn't want to add just a pool to their current yard. They wanted an entirely new space where they could entertain all of their (many) friends, and they wanted that new space to include a vanishing-edge pool, an outdoor kitchen with both a barbecue and a smoker, a spacious dining table, and a lounge area. Their goal was to create a space that would be perfect for hosting game-day parties and watching TV outdoors.

After listening to them talk about what they really wanted out of their backyard and then assessing their outdoor space, Paul realized that, because their house had been built on a slope, the best way to include everything they asked for was to raise the entire outdoor living area eight feet. That would give him room to incorporate multiple zones with plenty of entertainment and lounge space—perfect for those parties his clients were already looking forward to hosting.

The project Paul prepared for his clients after their initial meeting included a couple of extra surprises that he had planned for them, like that raised entertainment space that would make the most out of their sloped yard. It also pushed their original $120,000 budget closer to $200,000. But Paul wasn't worried that he had included too much in his design: his clients had been clear about what they wanted. Even if they decided to build just part of his design, Paul knew that they would want to see everything they'd asked for during their conversation, so he felt confident that he had made the right decision in adding those extras to his design.

That decision proved to be the right one. As his clients began to explore the interactive 3D presentation of their new space at their next meeting, they took notice of everything he had included: the spacious outdoor kitchen, the raised entertainment zones, and the extensive children's play area. They told Paul that they loved each and every feature.

To whet their appetite, Paul had emailed Jason and Jennifer a few photos before that meeting. His strategy worked: so tempted were they by those images he had shared in advance that they were eager to delve into the details. They liked his plans so much that even the new, higher price wasn't a deterrent: they were prepared to negotiate. As they went over the plans and the numbers together, they kept asking him to find another way to lower the price. To show them that he was already offering them the best possible price for what they wanted, Paul shared with them not just the detailed costs but also his own precise profit margins. Short of eliminating features or designing the project in phases, he told them, there was nothing else he could do to lower the cost.

To his surprise, his clients—adamant that they wanted the

design he'd presented to them—decided instead on a third solution: Jason, a doctor at the local hospital, would simply work more hours for a couple of months to make up the $80,000 difference between their budget and the design they wanted.

Their decision surprised Paul, who felt he had offered them multiple solutions that seemed far easier than working overtime for months. They were not interested, however, in changing anything. They didn't want to lower the custom raised layout, they didn't want to downsize the extensive outdoor kitchen, and they certainly didn't want to make any part of the project smaller than it was: "We have to have it like this," Jason said. "We want it to look exactly like the pictures."

Only after the couple had committed to working extra hours to afford the perfect outdoor living space did they share with Paul why they were so resolved to build the project exactly as he had presented it to them. Jason and Jennifer were both avid social media users, and they had already posted those first design screenshots that Paul had sent them before their second meeting. Their friends had immediately—and enthusiastically—chimed in to tell them how much they loved the plans.

In posting online those first enticing photos, Jason and Jennifer had done more than just share a couple of interesting pictures with their friends. Before they even saw Paul's full presentation, they had emotionally connected with his plans. Jennifer's feed had quickly filled with comments: her friends, asking when they were going to throw their first party, told her that they couldn't wait for football season so that they could all watch the game at their house. The enthusiasm that their family and friends expressed encouraged them to choose Paul's design. It was even worth working extra hours, Jason and Jennifer decided, so that they could enjoy with their friends the perfect space that they had already unveiled on social media.

Connecting Online—and in the Real World

When Paul's clients shared the photos of his design with their friends, they initially wanted simply to share their excitement. In posting photos online, they were in good company: according to Facebook, people share hundreds of millions of photos daily.[17] If they had chosen to share their project on Instagram instead, Jason and Jennifer would have joined the ranks of the hundreds of millions of monthly users who—according to the site's statistics—are not just willing to share photos. A majority of those users are also quite willing to interact with businesses on the network.[18] Whether searching for a business's hours, learning more about what a company can offer, or even just scrolling to see if the company has shared any cute new photos of the office dog, many readily turn to social media not just to see and post photos but also to get quick answers to their questions.

The ease with which social media users like Jason and Jennifer can instantly share photos and videos is due in part to the considerable effort companies like Facebook, Instagram, and Twitter have dedicated to making the sharing process feel completely painless. In fact, much like the story of Microsoft's founding—which famously began in a tiny garage—the stories of how each social media network began often involve entrepreneurs dedicating long hours to achieving their vision. Instead of garages, they often began in apartments and dorm rooms. And like Tennessee Williams, who dedicated his evenings to writing after working his day job, Instagram's Kevin Systrom, too, is said to have worked in marketing during the day while teaching himself to code at night.

Fifteen years after Mark Zuckerberg reportedly spent long hours in his dorm room working on what would eventually become Facebook, social media has become so ubiquitous that not only do users share hundreds of millions of photos daily, but researchers have also found that a significant majority of Americans get their news from social media.[19] Numerous researchers studying the impact of social media on purchasing decisions have found a significant, measurable effect at every stage of the customer "journey."[20]

These numbers reveal a remarkable shift over a short period of time—and also suggest how challenging it can be to avoid social media entirely. Sites like Facebook have become so popular, according to the Pew Research Center, that in little more than a decade, social media usage has jumped from 1 out of 20 Americans to nearly 7 out of 10.[21] People of all backgrounds and from all socioeconomic groups use one form of social media or another. And while Facebook, with its more than two billion users,[22] is one of the largest social media networks, it is just one of the many options available to users who want to share and connect.

In countless glowing press releases and blog posts, each one of the main social media sites—including Facebook, Instagram, Pinterest, Twitter, and even LinkedIn—has offered detailed statistics about just how much time users spend sharing information, images, videos, and messages. Taken as a whole, their statistics invite a promising question: given how much time users spend on social media, what content are they choosing to share?

As Paul, the pool builder in Texas, has learned, the answer to that question presents a remarkable opportunity for designers who want to build a solid relationship with their clients.

Setting Trends and Making Friends...
On and Off Social Media

One of the first well-known landscape designers—the eighteenth-century landscape architect, Lancelot "Capability"

Brown—might have relished the opportunity to share his work more broadly on social media.

A prolific designer, Brown is known for his work on numerous British estates, many of which are still well-known today—including Highclere Castle, better known as the setting of the popular TV series, *Downton Abbey*. His designs were sometimes so extensive that he had more than one village moved (a feat he and his clients would undertake at least in part to improve the view).[23] So popular were Brown's designs that, in 2016, gardens and museums in Britain marked the tercentenary of his birth with walks, exhibits, lectures, and games.[24]

One frequent feature of Brown's landscapes makes them seem ready-made for social media: the eye-catching details (sometimes called "illusions") he liked to include. Long before Brown began to share his landscaping ideas, it was common to visit and view gardens and estates from horseback as well as carriages. For example, Celia Fiennes, a seventeenth-century travel writer, wrote at length of the places she saw, heard, and even smelled while traveling on horseback. One garden grotto, she wrote, was "designed for diversion": it was "so contrived in one room [that] it makes [the] melody of Nightingerlls and all sorts of birds [which] engages [the] Curiosity of [the] Strangers to go in to see."[25] Sometimes what she was able to see, however, was limited by what her horse would tolerate: the smell of one place she visited was "so strong and offen[s]ive" that she "could not [force her] horse neare it."[26] Because visitors as well as owners would often view landscapes from horseback, Brown featured in his designs elaborate grottos or even small Greek temples—the likes of which can still be seen in television dramas and movies today—for them to enjoy as they, like Fiennes, explored the grounds.

That Brown's landscape designs are still enjoyed and even celebrated three hundred years after his birth is a remarkable achievement. His ideas grew so popular that he is said to have "altered in some way or other half the gardens in the country. He became the fashion, and was consulted by nearly [everyone] in England who had a garden of any consideration."[27] Famous painters like JMW Turner were even inspired by landscapes that Brown designed.[28] In the years since, his work has been recognized for the significant influence his ideas had on the developing field of landscape design.

Brown's landscapes appealed to his clients because he had a knack for combining practical solutions with excellent views—views that were not just impressive but also were expertly designed to earn notice. His designs—which stood as inspiration for many other estates—were more than merely practical or merely beautiful. He would sometimes build an extensive series of useful drains, for example.[29] He was also known for creating visually immersive optical illusions—like rivers that seemed to stretch on at considerable length when in fact they did not.[30]

Brown was able to design such large-scale landscapes in part because he had established a network of well-connected friends.[31] Of course, no matter how strong a network he created, even Brown—the man whose work was so well-loved that Horace Walpole, a famous author of the time, referred to him as "Lady Nature's second husband"[32]—had to persuade his clients to accept his plans. He was helped in large part by people, like Walpole, who wrote approvingly of Brown's work. In 1751, for example, Walpole wrote that an estate he'd visited had been "well laid out by one Brown": "the view pleased me more than I can express; the river Avon tumbles down a cascade at the foot of it." He added, "One sees what the prevalence of taste does."[33] Although Walpole wrote letters in the eighteenth century, not social media posts, his comments were frequently shared as widely then as many an online influencer's comments and posts are today.

Sharing a Good Story...in Real Life

Like any modern designer, Brown was also a talented storyteller—one who would visit his clients' estates to present his plans to them in just the right surroundings. In order to earn a commission, he would win over the owner of the house with a detailed and inspiring story that did more than just weave together all of the elements of his design. In discussing the existing environment and his plans to improve it, he emphasized how his design would benefit his clients and how he would create for his clients a beautiful view for them to enjoy.[34]

His strategy was so well known that one of the most well-known poets of the time, William Cowper, detailed in a poem what took place once "[t]he omnipotent magician, Brown" arrived at an estate:

> *He speaks. The lake in front becomes a lawn,*
> *Woods vanish, hills subside, and valleys rise,*
> *And streams, as if created for his use,*
> *Pursue the track of his directed wand*
> *Sinuous or straight, now rapid and now slow,*
> *Now murmuring soft, now roaring in cascades,*
> *Even as he bids. The enraptured owner smiles.*
> *'Tis finished.*[35]

Brown, like Paul in Texas, understood just how key it was to tell clients a great story. First, he would whet the client's appetite with great visuals. Then, he would draw them into the story by revealing how the design plans were created specifically for the client to enjoy with their friends and family. Finally, the "enraptured" clients would smile. That strategy has worked for nearly three centuries.

One reason why that strategy has been so successful for so long is that it proves to the client that the designer truly understands their needs—and has designed a plan with those needs in mind. Equally important, the strategy builds on a client's familiarity with their own property. Whether verbally sketching a plan while sitting astride a horse on a rolling estate or populating a 3D design with renderings of the client's own home, family dog, and favorite sports car, centering the client in their own familiar space before revealing new, perfectly suited improvements is an excellent way to build a compelling, personalized story.

Sharing a Good Story…on Social Media

One of the first steps in telling a good story is figuring out who the characters are and what they want.

Sometimes—like when Sean's client burst into happy tears when she saw his 3D design—the visual elements of the story are impressive enough that the client might not need to see a performative presentation as involved as Brown's. Brown, of course, didn't have modern 3D technology at his disposal as he told his clients stories about how they would enjoy the views he was going to create for them.

With the benefit of the latest technology—including 3D renderings, virtual reality, and augmented reality—designers today sharing a story with their clients can use another trick of Brown's: including design elements as visual surprises that are perfectly suited to catch the client's eye. Choosing the right design elements that will suit the client and their family means paying careful attention to what the client shares about themselves and how they want to enjoy their outdoor living space—as well as to how they want their friends, family, and neighbors to see them.

Paul learned that firsthand with his clients: in sharing photos of the future outdoor living space that Paul had designed, Jennifer hadn't just shared something she liked with her friends and family. She'd presented a "curated" version of her life—one that she wanted to share and enjoy with her friends.

That tendency to "curate" one's life online is familiar to many users. Even Google has described itself as a curator when highlighting its own research. It doesn't simply link to its research. Instead, Google invites viewers to "Discover our Curated Insights," where carefully selected information is beautifully arranged.[36] In fact, in his book *Everybody Lies*, Seth Stephens-Davidowitz makes the case that Facebook is perhaps inevitably the place where most of us at least *slightly* shade the truth about our lives. While social media networks like Facebook would have us believe that using real names and friending or following real people means we are in fact our "real" selves online, researchers (including Stephens-Davidowitz as well as numerous others) have found that most people present just a version of themselves on social media—one that is often both aspirational and very carefully managed.

Lancelot Brown and Paul from Texas make the case that these aspirational selves can be positively motivating rather than negative. For clients like Jennifer, the outdoor living space that Paul offered was so motivating, and the story of how she and her family would enjoy their new space with their friends so compelling, that, while she and her husband didn't need to go to quite the same lengths that the owners of the estates Brown renovated did—they certainly didn't need to relocate an entire village to achieve their goals—Jason and Jennifer were willing to prioritize making that design plan a reality.

Asking Better Questions: What Science Reveals

Whether telling a story directly to the client or indirectly for social media, getting to know a client well enough to frame their story successfully is both an art and a science. As Merve Emre, a professor at Oxford University, has suggested in her research into familiar personality assessments, tests, and quizzes, it took more than an adherence to the scientific method to create those now-familiar tests.[37] Getting to know a person, after all, is not the same as examining a slide under a microscope.

Numerous researchers studying the science of personality have explored how the familiar concept of a *story* can reveal important information about an individual. One such researcher, Northwestern University psychology professor Dan McAdams, developed one well-known approach to examining how we come to understand one another. His research reveals three levels to how people share information about themselves (and learn about other people); each level adds nuance and detail. It is not until the third level has been reached that a person's story is revealed.[38]

On social media, users often include brief—and frequently humorous—autobiographies or statements about themselves. These statements might reveal the first two layers discussed by McAdams. Even the friendliest and most unguarded among us, however, might not see social media status updates as a reflection of one's innermost identity—just as even the friendliest homeowners might not immediately see a casual conversation about what they want to do with their yard as an opportunity to open up about their hopes and dreams. That's one reason why it's important to ask good, meaningful questions.

One researcher, Arthur Aron, published a list of thirty-six now-famous questions intended to help people get to know each other. While numerous newspaper article writers and college course participants have reported back on just how successful these thirty-six questions are in fostering intimacy, few casual experimenters have taken the second step of also answering the list of "small-talk" questions Aron and his fellow researchers included in their study. These small-talk questions, designed for the researchers to test their own results, gave them the opportunity to determine whether the specific thirty-six questions they'd devised were truly what created intimacy when their study participants chatted. As anyone who has had to make unwanted small talk before surely recognizes, the carefully constructed set of questions generated far more interesting results than the small-talk ones did.

Aron's questions—which are intended to create a closer relationship than that which typically exists between a designer and a homeowner—provide some interesting insights into just how important knowing how to ask good questions really is.[39] According to Aron, it's not just that the thirty-six questions ask people to disclose personal information. Just as making small talk doesn't suffice to foster a collaborative relationship, neither does leaping straight into highly personal questions too quickly. The questions developed by Aron and his fellow researchers seem to work in part because they increase in intimacy gradually, leading the participants to willingly share with one another.

For designers seeking to build stronger communication with clients, Aron's experiment offers an important clue to how to ask questions that garner the best response from new acquaintances. When meeting with a new client, it's important to do more than just ask questions. To build trust, take the time to listen attentively so that you will be able to strike the right balance between making small talk and asking your client to open up to you about what they want most.

The 80-inch Flat Screen: Making Better Decisions, Faster

Although the next logical step after learning about your client's preferences and creating a design that will suit them might traditionally be "persuading the client to build the project," shifting expectations and norms mean that many clients now do a fair amount of online research before hiring a professional. They sometimes also have high expectations of just how easy it should be to conduct the purchasing process online—including reaching customer service and even getting quick estimates. One way to reduce potential friction that might slow down or stall the decision-making process is to consider how and why people sometimes hesitate to make decisions—even when they have considerable (and detailed) information at hand.

Designer Jim Bellamy, who began designing at 19 with pencil on vellum, recognizes how important it is to manage potential friction in the decision-making process when presenting to clients. His company—which has built more than 60,000 pools in California since 1952—has attained a 75% closing ratio in part because he and his team stay focused on making sure their clients enjoy a truly exceptional experience at every stage of the process.

They offer far more than a free bottle of water or a cup of coffee when welcoming clients to their office. After clients arrive at their private design center, they experience what Jim describes as a 4D presentation. He begins by showing them the 3D plans he has designed on an 80-inch flat-screen television while also sharing with them samples of tiles and pavers that they can touch.

"All of the materials that would be in Pool Studio on the screen are actually there to touch and feel," Jim says. Having samples available helps his clients not just see but also feel exactly what he will build for them, creating a far more immersive experience.

So positively do his clients respond to and enjoy his interactive presentations that Jim says, "If I had to go back to 2D drawing, I'd go sell cars or something because [3D] is such an amazing tool."

The thoughtful design center that Jim and his team have created is more than just a place for his clients to see their future outdoor living spaces. "I design the dream," Jim says. "I draw everything. I don't just draw the pool. I draw the entire backyard."

In doing so, Jim helps his clients understand how each and every piece of his design works together to give them exactly what they want. He doesn't expect his clients to know how many square feet of deck they need. Instead, he asks them how many people they expect to host at their next party. Then, "after the presentation starts," he explains, "they hardly ever look at me."

That's because it isn't just seeing a design on an 80-inch screen that motivates Jim's clients. It's seeing their own home, and feeling emotionally connected to the space Jim and his team have created, that inspires his clients. One of those clients, who came to Jim after meeting with five or six other builders, even began to cry with relief after seeing the interactive 4D presentation of the design that he created for her: "She said, 'I'm going to do this because now I know what I'm going to get.'"

Studying the processes people use to make decisions—like what motivated Paul's clients to post online or how Jim's clients choose between samples—reveals interesting insights into just how quickly people make decisions, and just how much those decisions can be influenced (and improved).

Reducing Friction on Social Media

Social media networks reduce friction by making it nearly effortless to share photos, post updates, and respond to one another: apps open at a touch, images upload easily, and friends get to see what we're seeing—instantly.

And, of course, sharing thoughts and experiences on social media doesn't happen in a vacuum. Social media users engage with one another's posts and photos—sometimes with comments, sometimes with likes, and sometimes by taking action.

Like Zuckerberg's fellow classmates, who liked to find out who was taking which class before signing up for their own classes, many social media users like to check out what their friends and family have to say before making decisions.

We're often motivated to buy things because our friends like them—and to undertake large-scale landscape design projects because our friends approve. That is true to such an extent that, today, researchers are finding that people are even more likely to turn to social media for feedback than previously anticipated.[40]

Getting Clients Great Feedback

The successful impact of Jennifer's project images reveals more than one important detail about how social media users share information about themselves online. Not only do people like to share current information online with family and friends who know them offline, and not only do people enjoy sharing photos and videos, but people also take action based on feedback from their friends and followers.

For designers—especially for designers who want to build solid relationships with their prospective clients—the details of how people connect with and respond to one another are well worth exploring. Some researchers—like Seth Stephens-Davidowitz, who has gathered stats on how people *actually* spend time online (compared to how they say they are going to spend their time)—take care to point out that social media usage can have some drawbacks.

The tendency to compare ourselves to our peers is one of the drawbacks often identified by researchers in articles published on the topic of social media. However, the ubiquity of social media is such that even the most cautionary articles appear on-screen right alongside quick-and-easy Facebook and Twitter buttons, making the article easy to share on the very same social media networks that the article is cautioning against. As aware as we might be of the fact that the people we follow online are likely choosing to share just the best moments of their lives, we often still want to keep up with what our friends and family are doing. Even if we know that the Joneses are sharing just their own highlight reel, we still judge ourselves—quite harshly—against their visible successes. Sharing truly meaningful experiences—for example, the story of how the new pool will be the place where friends and family enjoy wonderful summer afternoons together—is one way to help make those online conversations feel genuinely meaningful, too. The pool is more than just a beautiful addition to the home, just as the landscaping is more than just something for the mower to navigate around. The experiences the family will share and enjoy are what truly matter.

Designers can make the most of social media by helping people connect to their loved ones and share what's truly important with them. Helping clients get encouraging feedback will, both directly and indirectly, help them feel confident that they're not just choosing the best project. They're also choosing the project that they (and their family) will enjoy the most. As Paul's experience sharing images of his design with Jennifer and Jason shows, even simply offering clients a couple of pictures and videos that are ready to share on social media is an easy way to help clients engage with their friends and family as they commit to a design project.

What Makes People Tick?

Engaging both clients and their friends in the decision-making process sometimes works so smoothly that you, like Paul, might not find out that social media helped a project along until the client is ready to sign the contract.

Even a cursory glance at data on the customer decision-making process reveals that old-fashioned advertising has had to make room for a more collaborative, engaging approach. Sometimes, as a client is making those myriad decisions along the path to building a project, they need a little extra help. Maybe they need reassurance that the project really will give them what they want. Maybe they worry about picking just the right finishes. As a survey conducted by social media site Houzz found, while many homeowners end up hiring professional help, significantly fewer initially *intend* to hire outside help.[41]

Combining stories, visuals, and social media to help clients on the decision-making "journey" feel more confident is one collaborative approach—and one way to make that collaboration with clients even more successful is to draw on lessons that Google shared after analyzing why some teams achieved notably better results than others.

What makes a team successful?

In 2012, Google set out to answer a question that has challenged anyone who has ever collaborated on a project: what makes a good team tick? To find out, they began to research how people worked together—and what made some teams measurably more successful than others.

During an earlier study, codenamed Project Oxygen, Google had analyzed whether managers were even necessary. The short answer (spoiler alert): yes. While many tech companies—Google among them—sometimes prioritize technical skills in the hiring process, research has revealed that tech skills alone are not the key to success. In fact, in Google's study, tech skills weren't even at the top of the list. It took much more than sheer genius or the highest grades to rank among the most successful. So-called "soft" skills—like empathy—were vital.

The question Google was researching was not a new one. Decades before Google's research team shared their findings, Dale Carnegie identified much the same results in his now-classic *How to Win Friends and Influence People*. Carnegie didn't title his book, *How to Win More Contracts*, or *How to Be More Productive*. The title he chose provides more than a hint at his conclusion. Carnegie, like Google, understood that knowledge and technical skills alone were not enough. He recognized that being able to deal capably with other people was vitally important—and his book has remained a bestseller because his tips on how to do so are still relevant and useful today.

Of course, it's possible to be the best at what you do and be very good at building excellent relationships and still sometimes fail to reach your goals. That lesson is one reflected in another source that has attained similar long-standing acclaim: *Star Trek*. It is one of many life lessons taught by Captain Jean-Luc Picard—and it is perhaps one reason why so many people from so many different backgrounds cite that long-running show as an inspiration, just as so many respond to Carnegie's advice.

While television space captains and elementary school teachers alike might agree on the value of learning from failure and continuing to try one's best, it's admittedly unlikely that anyone outside of a satirical movie about corrupt theater producers would *deliberately* set out to fail. Today, that need to balance technical skills with people skills is one reason why many companies dedicate significant time and resources not just to technical training but also to the development of "softer" skills. For many companies, that includes bolstering their social media strategy to make it easier to build better relationships with clients.

How to Balance Skills

Figuring out how to best use social media to connect with clients—including not just Facebook but also other networks like Twitter, Instagram, and YouTube—is an achievement that many companies find difficult to master. Even as many businesses turn to social media, few companies actively train their sales teams in social selling.

Sometimes, recommendations on how to build a good reputation online or how to connect with customers come in the form of a pithy quote from a famous athlete like Wayne Gretzky or politician like JFK. Or, perhaps, the recommendations come alongside an admonishment to use big data. After all, who doesn't have an in-house statistician ready to "drill down" into the data?

As Dale Carnegie, *Star Trek*, and Google all suggest, it's not enough to have just the data or the tech skills or even the genius design skills. Designing great projects, frankly, is just one piece of the puzzle. Reaching clients, and helping them emotionally connect to your great design, is vital. And social media has grown into more than just a way to connect with prospective clients and strengthen relationships with current clients. It's increasingly important that small businesses and small business owners think strategically about how to use social media because social media is often how many consumers and homeowners first learn about what a company offers and then make purchasing decisions.

However, even the most established companies with the biggest social media budgets sometimes stumble when attempting to connect with clients. Facebook itself—the same company whose often-changing social media rules challenge companies to devise a rapidly changing response—has faced much the same challenge that Google, Captain Picard, and salespeople trying to perfect their social media approach have faced. And how

Facebook faced its own missteps offers designers a look at how "soft" people skills can help make a team more successful.

News Feed: The Feature that Earned 100,000 Protests

Today, Facebook's News Feed is an integral part of the service. When it was introduced in 2006, however, it was so instantly unpopular that articles detailing the user response immediately sprang up. The same day that the News Feed launched, 100,000 people joined a Facebook Group protesting it.[42]

The response to the launch of News Feed apparently came as a surprise to the company, which seemed to have expected its users to enjoy the new format. According to Facebook, the feed was meant to look as familiar—and as mundane—as a newspaper. Indeed, Facebook saw the News Feed as an improvement to the service it provided its users. Instead of having to click on each friend's page to see what they were up to, a user could see all of their friends' updates in one place.

Where it stumbled was in communicating that benefit to its users. However, that stumble did not prevent Facebook from attaining its goal of using the News Feed to engage users with the site. Those 100,000 members who joined the protest group helped to spur engagement. As people signed in, they saw the news—and the protest—appear on their redesigned screens. The very existence of that protest group served to prove both the popularity and the functionality of the new feature.

Building People Skills

Whether you're selling nine million users on the News Feed or you're offering a family a brand-new swimming pool, you need more than just the expertise to create what you know will be an excellent option for your audience. You also need the people skills to help your clients understand why what you've created is perfect for them. Facebook would grow from a niche site for students at Harvard to a worldwide network—soon reaching what seemed like a groundbreaking nine million users before eventually reaching more than two billion users each month, at a time when, according to statisticians, just twice as many people as that used the internet[43]—in part because it rallied its team's "soft" skills (empathy, good communication, adaptability) to respond to its users and address missteps.

Of course, companies the size of Google and Facebook can afford to spend considerable money and resources training teams on how to develop these important "soft" skills. For smaller companies, handling social media and engaging with clients online can prove time consuming and expensive if not done strategically. That's why it's important to assess where your "soft" skills land relative to your design expertise.

As studies have shown, when it comes to communication, customer expectations have already been set, and clients expect to be able to find and reach businesses online. Large companies like Amazon, Apple, and Google can offer customer service experiences—complete, in some cases, with 24/7 customer service or an entire social media team standing ready to respond to any questions or complaints—that can seem out of reach for smaller businesses.

What Lancelot Brown and Paul from Texas—as well as Jean-Luc Picard and Facebook—have shown is that building excellent relationships and connecting with clients (in Brown's case, successfully enough to leave a legacy that is still celebrated nearly three hundred years later) means taking care to balance strong technical skills with excellent people skills. No matter how inspiring Brown's stories were, and no matter how trend-setting his landscape designs proved, he found his clients and he earned his recommendations in much the same way that Paul in Texas, centuries later, also earns his client referrals: through solid work and great word of mouth.

Key Takeaways

When meeting with clients who use social media, offering them easy-to-share images and engaging stories is a great way to both reveal your design and connect to clients where they already are: online.

- Clients expect to be able to research options online, so make yourself easy for them to find. Keep your information up to date so that leads will be motivated to contact you when they see what your company offers them.
- Reduce potential friction in the decision-making process by offering clients great visuals of their future outdoor living space that are easy for them to share with their friends and family online. You'll not just help them connect with your design. You'll also help them gain positive feedback from their friends and family.
- Improve your "soft" skills—like empathy—to bolster your strong technical and design skills.

THREE

YOU ARE THE EXPERT

Art does not reflect the visible,
but makes visible.
–Paul Klee[44]

THE GOAL THAT WON THE Chicago Blackhawks their first Stanley Cup in forty-nine years was one that, initially, nobody other than the player who had scored seemed to see. Even as an exuberant Patrick Kane skated back toward the rest of his team, the commentators were lagging a few seconds behind. Kane knew instantly that he'd made the shot, but the puck seemed to have disappeared from view. Viewers were able to spot it only on replay, after it was finally retrieved from under the net.

What was unmistakable—in the temporary absence of the puck—was Kane's own confidence. Everyone else needed a little help to see what he clearly knew would be a winning goal from the moment he shot it. In fact, even his own teammates seemed momentarily puzzled, if happy to celebrate the goal with him. They were equally enthusiastic as they reformed their celebratory pile when the temporarily missing puck was found.[45]

Given that a hockey puck measures just three inches in diameter and can travel at speeds of up to one hundred miles per hour in a game, keeping track of an object that small—that moves so quickly—takes some considerable skill.[46]

Kane is not the only star performer who seems to see what others—even teammates playing the same game—do not see in quite the same way, or at least do not see without a little extra help. When Mickey Mantle hit his legendary 565-ft home run in 1953, he famously compared the ball to a grapefruit.[47] And when Michelangelo wrote a sonnet on the artistic process, he commented on "all" that the artist had to do to sculpt a piece:

> *The best of artists hath no thought to show*
> *Which the rough stone in its superfluous shell*
> *Doth not include: to break the marble spell*
> *Is all the hand that serves the brain can do.*
> —Michelangelo, *Sonnet XV*[48]

In interviews, top-performing athletes like Kane sometimes echo Michelangelo's seemingly casual take on performance: "all" an artist has to do is break away that "marble spell," that "superfluous shell." Perhaps all a baseball player has to do is to—somehow—see that regulation ball the same size as a grapefruit. Or a hockey player "just" has to make a lucky shot that nobody else is quite fast enough to see, let alone block.

Being able to zero in on a 3-inch hockey puck zipping across the ice, a 9-inch baseball moving just as fast, or an 18-inch basketball hoop 10 feet in the air can seem to require nearly as much skill, dedication, and talent as it took Michelangelo to "see" a sculpture before he even began.

The ability to see a grapefruit instead of a regulation 9-inch baseball—or to know the puck has made it in when everyone else is seconds behind—can indeed sometimes seem a matter more of exceptional luck than anything else. That is why researchers studying athletic performance have long been intrigued by exactly what it is that truly drives exceptional performance. Seeing that grapefruit of a baseball or that "superfluous shell" around a sculpture takes far more than just an instinctive good eye. Learning to "see" what others don't is a skill like any other—one that requires training, practice, and, perhaps equally important, confidence.

That same skill is how designers know a design is going to work, long before the homeowners themselves can see how their yard will be transformed—and maybe even before the designer's own team has fully grasped exactly how the transformation will work.

The Pool on the Cliff

Coordinating projects that go beyond the "builder's special" takes considerable skill and experience, whether that project is a pool for a multilevel yard, a social-media-ready pool built in time for a client's next party, or a landscape renovation that seems to keep changing in size and scope.

Research conducted by the social media site Houzz has confirmed what many designers likely already know: of the homeowners surveyed, significantly more ended up hiring a professional than originally planned to. One reason is that, sometimes, when a family intends to do the work themselves with a DIY renovation, they discover midcourse that they still really do need a designer and a builder.

Other projects, however, are so big and so daunting that it takes just the right designer to figure out how to deliver the impressive results the clients want. Being able to see what others could not yet see is how Barry Justus built a grand slam of a design for clients whose outdoor living space had proven to be a remarkable challenge even before Justus was consulted. He was asked to create a design that was both literally and figuratively groundbreaking.

His field wasn't an ice rink, and it wasn't a baseball diamond. In fact, it wasn't a field or even a lawn at all. It was a location so imposing that his first visit to the site inspired both "fear and awe": a house on a granite cliff.[49]

That sense of anticipation was amplified by the fact that there were ten feet of snow on the ground the first time Justus visited the site. The house—a large country estate colloquially known as a "cottage"—was located in a pristine, protected corner of Canada where Justus (one hundred fifty miles from his own home turf) knew that protecting the environment would take priority and also that he and his team, as outsiders, would have to tread carefully when approaching local building officials.

Every detail had to be planned out carefully in advance, both for the client's approval and for the long list of necessary permits. By hiring as many local experts and subcontractors as possible, Justus demonstrated respect for local concerns while also relying on the valuable expertise each local brought to the job—an especially important consideration given the "extremely accurate measurements"[50] that Justus knew were necessary for a successful project. As Justus recognized, coordinating a large team under such strict conditions took many of the "soft" skills that Google's research revealed to be equally as important as—and sometimes even more important than—technical expertise.

It wasn't just a matter of hiring the right team, either. The location meant that Justus also had to coordinate housing and meals while still minimizing the impact on the local environment. With the understanding that "a construction crew is a bit like an army, and an army runs on its stomach," he even hired "a local gourmet restaurant to cater lunches and dinners."[51]

Achieving a project of that size, at that scale, and under those constraints required a deft hand. The location—where they needed to carefully blast granite bedrock one hundred thirty feet above the frozen lake while minimizing any impact on the environment—offered very little room for error. And that razor-thin margin for error required Justus and his team to communicate and check in daily to handle everything from parking to on-site food storage. The site sometimes looked, Justus says, "like an anthill."[52] They weren't just blasting granite to install a pool. They were also building a sports court, cantilevered decks, and a lounging area—while making sure that the entire project complemented and protected both the natural environment and the cottage itself. To handle that much activity on such narrow roads, they even temporarily installed portable traffic lights. And to prevent bears from approaching, they had to strictly remove and secure all food waste from the property.

"The sheer scope of the project combined with the steep-sloped property and the overriding environmental concerns" meant that "the level of detail in the design work was staggering. Every light, drain, electrical conduit, and stone pattern needed to be plotted, installed, and checked," according to Justus, not only so that the client could approve the plans and choose materials but also so that the team could make sure the build went smoothly.[53]

Being able to look at a cliff and conceptualize not just the pool perched atop it but also all the work required to build that pool and suspended sports court is how Barry Justus and his team achieved spectacular results. Along the way, they managed everything from permits to hotels, traffic lights to bears. Months of careful, coordinated effort prepared them to handle any issues that cropped up. Their careful planning even extended beyond the build itself: they installed a remote monitoring system that made it easy for Barry and his team to stay ahead of any minor issues that required attention. The system they chose also provided the client with the ability to use an app to do things like heat up the spa while en route to the cottage.

Of course, long before Barry was able to offer that app to his client, he and his team needed to show the client that they were going to be able to build him exactly what he wanted. The sheer size of the project required that Barry find new ways to help his client understand the exceptionally detailed and precise site plans.

Marilyn Einstein or Albert Monroe?

In a magazine article or on a waiting room wall, you've likely encountered an optical illusion challenge. Perhaps you studied one featured in a self-assessment quiz.

In one well-known optical illusion created by MIT professor Aude Oliva, Marilyn Monroe's face appears to morph into none other than Albert Einstein's.[54] While it's true that both Monroe and Einstein were famous for their distinctive light-colored hair, it is only a trick of the light—and some very carefully chosen filters—that transforms Monroe's glossy curls into Einstein's untamed style, and her smile into his mustache.

In another famous optical illusion, two faces appear to mirror each other, even as the negative space between the faces reveals itself as a vase.

What you see when looking at one of those optical illusions—and how quickly you see it—can depend on a number of factors, including your vision (for example, if you're farsighted or nearsighted). Consider, for example, the following 2D illustration. What do you see?

At trade shows, many seasoned designers have come up with a surprisingly wide variety of answers when presented with that drawing—everything from a donut with a handle to a pool float.

Viewed from another angle, the object under consideration becomes clear: it's a coffee cup.

Of course, once you've seen it, the optical illusion is fleeting: it disappears the instant you recognize what you're seeing. Once you know the "trick," you can see both the mirrored faces and the vase. You can squint to morph Einstein's face into Monroe's. Or you can see that donut become a coffee cup. Slowed down and zoomed in, the path of Mantle's baseball or Kane's puck becomes easy for anyone to trace and follow. With the mystery gone, you know exactly what it is that you're really looking for—and seeing.

For many designers, pool and landscape plans are a bit like those optical illusions: once you know how to look at them, you always know what you're seeing. For homeowners, however, these images are brand new—and often just as incomprehensible as an optical illusion before the visual "trick" becomes clear. For many, staring down at a 2D drawing of their yard is exactly like seeing an image of an idiosyncratically coiffed scientist and being asked to find a glamorous movie star: even if told that the image is going to morph and transform, they don't yet know how to see it.

As entertaining as such optical illusions are, other examples reveal startling facts about just how wide that perception gap can be. For example, according to the Department of Transportation's Federal Highway Administration, there were 218 million licensed drivers in the US as of 2015. Not only do more than eight out of ten people of driving age have a license, but those 218 million people also cover a lot of distance—measured at more than three trillion miles, in fact.[55]

Given how much time Americans spend on the road, it would be easy to assume that most are familiar with one of the most common features on the road—the dashed lines. However, repeated studies done by researcher Dennis Shaffer have found that most people have no idea how long those dashed lines actually are. Not only that, but their estimates are often startlingly inaccurate: in his study, participants regularly guessed that the dashed road lines and the length of the gaps between the road lines were just a fraction of what they really are.[56]

Dr. Shaffer's study raises an idea with intriguing implications for designers to consider: the seemingly clear and straightforward math that designers, engineers, architects, and builders use to build not just roads but also other outdoor spaces might not appear quite so straightforward to other viewers. That applies as much to homeowners viewing a new design as to the participants in the professor's study.[57]

Given that so many people are unable to recognize the true size and scale of something as familiar as the dashed lines on a road, it's not surprising that many homeowners struggle to understand how less familiar features and materials will look in their own space. Without help, a homeowner might not be able to grasp what is truly possible to achieve in their outdoor living design.

Wax Models, Horseback Tours, and 3D Renderings: How to Communicate Innovative Ideas

As Barry Justus knew long before his first meeting at his client's house on the cliff, being able to communicate plans clearly enough for a client to not just understand what is being offered but to also eagerly anticipate the finished results is key to a smooth, successful design and build.

While Lancelot Brown could often convince his clients of the value of his plans while touring the property on horseback, today most homeowners prefer a somewhat different—and often markedly more visually detailed—approach. In fact, even Michelangelo's clients occasionally wanted proof that he could deliver what they were commissioning him to create. His small wax models—some of which still survive today—are an intriguing precursor to the 3D models that today's designers use to share ideas with clients.

His wax models were more than just proof of concept offered to a client. They were also an important part of Michelangelo's design process. It's owing to Michelangelo's fame that some of his wax models survive—and to his biographer, Giorgio Vasari, that we understand the intriguing manner in which Michelangelo used those models when chiseling away the "superfluous shell" of his chosen marble.

Described by Vasari as the process of "how to carve figures from the marble by a method secure from any chance of spoiling the stone," Michelangelo's process was intriguing:

> *You take a figure in wax or some other solid material, and lay it horizontally in a vessel of water, which water being by its nature flat and level at the surface, as you raise the said figure little by little from the level, so it comes about that the more salient parts are revealed, while the lower parts–those, namely, on the underside of the figure–remain hidden, until in the end it all comes into view. In the same manner must figures be carved out of marble with the chisel, first laying bare the more salient parts, and then little by little the lower parts.*[58]

Like Michelangelo, Justus relied upon precise scaled renderings of his design to plan the details and to reveal to the client the nature of those details. As the project was built, bit by bit, the client could see how it matched the 3D design that had attracted him to Justus's ideas for the property—much as the "salient parts" of Michelangelo's model would also be gradually revealed until the full project was complete.

Of course, as anyone who has tried to navigate a funhouse or figure out the trick to an optical illusion recognizes, even seemingly clear images—be they a picture of a vase that resolves itself into two mirrored faces or funhouse mirrors that turn out to not reflect reality quite as we expect it—can still present a unique challenge to the viewer.

Establishing expertise in the eyes of the client obviously takes more than a list of accolades or even a great portfolio of images. Not even Michelangelo or Lancelot Brown could always win a commission on the strength of reputation alone. That is why—for designers, builders, and artists alike—being able to communicate, listen, and share ideas clearly is about more than just creating a beautiful rendering or well-told story. It actually requires many of the "soft" skills that Google identified as integral to any successful team undertaking. Proving one's expertise means understanding just what it is that a client really wants, and then sharing the answer to those needs and wants in a way that the client can in turn understand—whether through a wax model, a 3D rendering, or a beautiful story.

Doing so successfully requires a bit more legwork than some of the most frequently shared sales tips would suggest. While some designers very successfully use social media sites (like Houzz and Pinterest) to help clients brainstorm ideas, just asking the client *"what do you want?"* and merely glancing together at some photos found online is, frankly, not an especially productive approach. It might even be a waste of time.

Designer Shane LeBlanc points out one reason why: sometimes, the reason why a client likes or saves a photo is not immediately obvious. He takes care to ask his clients questions about the images they choose because he has noticed that, occasionally, it is not the shape of the pool in the photo, for example, that catches their eye. It's the pillow cushions.

Of course, just as clients aren't buying pools because they're so impressed by the shotcrete specs, clients aren't really paying for just the concrete, steel, glass, or even pillow cushions that make up the necessary details of the installed project any more than they're paying a designer to just replicate another project they might have spotted on social media. Most homeowners want unique, personalized projects that do more than just check off a list of basics or even must-haves—like Sean's design, which moved his client to tears of joy, or Paul's, which inspired his clients to add hours to their work schedules to meet the budget.

When buying and selling art, the technical specs often seem almost irrelevant to the ultimate value of the painting. Contemporary artists sometimes sell art for mind-boggling sums—sums that are typically unrelated to the actual cost of the materials involved. And, just like contemporary art buyers who might be more interested in the history and provenance of a work than in the technical details of exactly which brand of paint was chosen or brushes were used, many homeowners are typically far more interested in achieving and enjoying unique and innovative spaces than they are in learning the technical details of just how those innovative features will get built.

To help a client make a decision about undertaking a unique renovation, it can be helpful to put to use findings from studies on how persuasion really works. Many people rely on shortcuts, or heuristics, to make better (and faster) decisions. And many don't find listening to a salesperson talk themselves up especially persuasive. What an expert designer can do, therefore, is put those "soft" skills to excellent use and take advantage of the intriguing studies that reveal how best to help indecisive clients make great decisions.

Sometimes, the value of implementing that research is vividly clear to see. For example, Robert Cialdini's exceptionally popular and lasting research into the science of persuasion has revealed that certain classic appeals—like the appeal to authority, for example—are really just one piece of the puzzle. It's often the seemingly minor details that make the biggest, most measurable difference.[59] In a presentation, details that are easy to add—like the family's name on a sign—can prove especially compelling.

Appeals to authority, however, have long been popular—and have been debated just as long. Even in the thirteenth century, Thomas Aquinas wrote at some length analyzing why "the proof from authority is the weakest form of proof."[60] One does not need to turn to Aquinas for the proof of that: any parent—or anyone who has watched a television sitcom—knows just how successful arguing *"because I said so"* is likely to be.

To some homeowners, the hard sell or the untempered appeal

to authority might feel about as persuasive as if a surgeon today were to follow the example of surgeons of centuries past and show up to a new patient's bedside wearing robes bloodstained from surgery, expecting those stains to stand as a testament to their experience and skill. And, just as the value of washing one's hands instead of displaying those stains is now well supported by science, the value of taking a strategic approach is equally supported by research.

Of course, the findings from some of those well-researched studies might require more time to implement than personalizing your client's presentation by simply adding their name to a welcoming sign. One such article worthy of consideration became so popular that the study has acquired an instantly recognizable and abbreviated title of its own—and the results of that study have proved so intriguing that they have influenced everyone from casual buyers to bankers, students to statisticians.

99 Bottles of Jam on the Wall: When *More* Becomes *Too Much*

When researcher Sheena Iyengar published the article that would soon become known as The Jam Study, she and her coauthor, Mark Lepper, did not anticipate it would become quite as popular as it did. The seemingly simple question that they were investigating, however, proved intriguing to many: was more *really* more?[61]

In their study, they tackled a topic that they noticed had gone overlooked. They realized that, although many of the published studies they were reading often assumed that it was better to have more choices, the studies they were reviewing tended to offer participants a limited number of choices: often, no more than six.[62]

To find out what would happen when study participants were offered even more of those seemingly desirable choices, they set up a series of experiments—including a grocery store display of jams that sometimes offered six options and sometimes twenty-four. Intriguingly, far more people bought jam when they saw fewer options: 30% vs. 3%.[63] (For those who don't want to break out a calculator: the jump from 3% to 30% is a rather remarkable 900% increase.) Even more intriguing: those who had faced down the large selection—not just of jams but also other choices offered in the experiments they conducted—seemed to struggle more to make a decision.[64]

Their answer—maybe more *wasn't* actually more—appealed to science journalists as much as to highly paid corporate consultants, psychology students as much as marketing analysts. And their research—published in the year 2000—has since inspired numerous other studies, experiments, and publications. Significant research has gone into analyzing the reasons why offering any specific number of choices at any given time will—or will not—work.

As the familiar story of Goldilocks suggests—and as numerous studies into choice theory confirm—sometimes *three* choices are, in fact, optimal. Whether offering good-better-best—like those three bears' three bowls of porridge in front of Goldilocks—or using the familiar "good, cheap, fast: choose any two" rubric to compare options, at least *one* of those three choices, the theory goes, will be just right.

Before a designer can ask a client which of any given set—three tile options for the pool, or three different types of pavers for the walkway—is "just right," it is a good idea to narrow down the options as much as possible. Doing so is far easier for the expert designer than it is for the client. For example, while children present at client meetings often get excited at the idea of an especially deep pool, the games they will actually enjoy playing (like volleyball or Marco Polo) are usually best suited to pools of slightly less dramatic depths.

For a family with kids who want to play games in the pool, designing a pool with extra steps and benches for them to enjoy and use in their games will ultimately be more appealing than just a "standard" rectangular pool with a depth of six feet (or approximately two meters). Children, of course, aren't alone in dreaming up features and ideas that ultimately aren't quite what they really want. One reason it is so important to understand how a family intends to enjoy their new space is that the ideal placement of new features can vary considerably, depending on the family's lifestyle.

A designer named Mike recently realized the importance of keeping track not just of what a client says they want from their outdoor space but also of what they share with him about how they use—or are going to use—their indoor living space. Mike's client was looking forward to enjoying outdoor meals under the new covered patio they were planning to add. However, Mike realized that the new pergola would partially block their view of the pool from the master bedroom. Since Mike remembered that the client had mentioned that they were going to start working from home at a newly installed, custom-made desk in their master suite—and that they were looking forward to being able to glance down and see their kids playing—Mike knew that he had to reconfigure their deck to give them the shade they wanted for early family dinners while also preserving the view from upstairs.

As Mike's experience highlights, it's important to learn about a family's day-to-day routine when planning an outdoor design. Thoughtful details—like preserving the view from the master suite, or situating a beautiful water feature so that it's visible from the den where the visiting grandparents like to sit and bird watch before starting their day—can transform a project and make it stand out from the rest.

As Barry Justus's meticulous 3D renderings proved, plotting out each and every detail—including each and every light, for example—can be the most efficient way to demonstrate why some options work better than others. After all, what might be intuitively obvious to a designer who is used to reading plans is not always obvious to a homeowner. And some homeowners like to study 3D plans to take in all of the details, just as some viewers of optical illusions enjoy pulling out a ruler to confirm that two given lines really are—or aren't!—the same length.

The gap that sometimes exists between what a client says they want to see in their yard versus what they describe when asked how they would like to enjoy their new yard is one reason many designers prefer not to design a new project directly in front of the clients. As easy as that is to do with user-friendly software, sometimes the wide array of options available—and therefore visible on-screen—can lead the client to feel like they are facing down far too many choices at once, making the experience frustrating rather than enjoyable.

Instead, one excellent way to involve the client in the design process is to follow the example of one internationally popular store, IKEA.

What's Mine is *Great:* Putting the IKEA Effect to Work

The average outdoor living project often involves quite a few necessary decisions—and even following the classic "good, better, best" approach to managing options can still risk overwhelming clients if those orderly sets of options just keep coming.

For designers and builders, even the most innovative projects in the most challenging locations (typically) follow a similar process. Whether or not there are bears to contend with, the steps involved in, say, measuring a pool are as familiar as analyzing dashed lines on a road would be for a traffic engineer or tracking a baseball game's stats for a dedicated fan.

For homeowners, however, thinking about undertaking a renovation project might seem a bit like leaping into the middle of an unfamiliar game—and trying to keep an eye not just on the fast-moving puck or 100-mph baseball but also on everything else going on, all at once. Studies looking at how people ascribe value to things offer one possible solution to helping clients feel great about the choices they need to make: help them feel like what is being created is *theirs*.

One such study was conducted by Michael Norton, Daniel Mochon, and Dan Ariely. In their paper, they analyze why it is that people value what they create so much that, sometimes, they value it *even more* than if it had been created by an "expert" alone. What they found, they deemed the IKEA Effect: people, it seems, really do place a high value on things that they themselves have created—or at least helped to create.[65]

Outdoor living designs, of course, are not quite as DIY-friendly as a bookcase or end table might be. Sometimes, it is true that clients are extremely happy with a project exactly as it is. So much so, that they want to build it *exactly* as it is presented. That's why Sean's client cried tears of joy on seeing her dream come alive in 3D and why Paul's clients were happy to schedule overtime so they could make sure their finished project included each and every detail they had admired during the presentation.

Many clients, however, want to make at least a few changes along the way. Some are like Barry Justus's clifftop cottage client—so pleased with the proposal that they are eager to expand the project. Taking the time to listen to and understand their goals, wants, and needs goes a long way toward making sure the presentation meets with their enthusiastic approval—whether the client is deciding to expand the project or just finalize a tile option. Of course, even when the thoughtfully told story of a presentation makes the homeowner eager to start building, the job, as it were, is only half done. The next step? Making sure the experience is as enjoyable as the presentation—and the finished results as incredible as hoped for.

Although most projects do not involve quite as many moving parts on quite as strict a timeline as Barry Justus's client's house on the cliff, even if a client's outdoor living project does not come with the risk of hungry bears nosing at forgotten leftovers, it likely involves far more of those "moving parts" than the homeowner anticipates. And, as Sheena Iyengar's Jam Study reveals, sometimes more can end up seeming like too much. Homeowners facing down seemingly limitless options might hesitate or even postpone a project.

Even when a client is certain that they want to build, they might not be able to readily grasp the benefits when exploring plans on their own. For a client who is contemplating a new pizza oven, for example, or comparing a negative-edge pool to a zero-edge one, the benefits of any given choice might not seem immediately clear. That is because—just like being able to "see" the trick of an optical illusion—just how "easy" some purportedly straightforward projects are depends on skill level, familiarity, and expertise. Projects that might be easy for an expert to execute sometimes prove surprisingly arduous for anyone else—while looking, notably, like they *ought* to be easy.

Of Mice and Math: When Surprises Aren't Ideal

When the team behind the popular educational program Jump Math analyzed why students struggle to solve math equations, they identified a common scenario that expert designers might recognize as readily as math teachers. As their research highlights, experts do not always immediately recognize why a concept is hard for non-experts to understand.[66] For a math teacher, it is second nature to solve complex equations that stretch to cover an entire classroom whiteboard. Students, however, might not immediately recognize or understand all of the steps that they need to take. Asking students to solve an unfamiliar equation without helping them see all of those "hidden" steps might be as fruitful as asking a client to triangulate a freeform pool. The client, like the student, might understand basic geometry. But being able to understand the necessary steps involved in, for example, triangulating a convex polygon—and why each step matters—takes both skill and training. Just like students who don't understand the steps involved in an equation aren't able to solve it, homeowners who can't quite "see" what they're looking at might, therefore, hesitate to make a decision.

And as Robert Burns wrote in 1785, even "the best laid plans of mice and men often go awry."[67] Even the best plans created by the most experienced designers sometimes meet with unexpected snags, delays, and surprises. Homeowners facing down these surprises might feel like stressed math students who aren't able to understand all of the steps that go into solving an equation. A homeowner might be quite happy with a "some assembly required" bookshelf or chair—no matter how it turns out—for the simple reason that they built it. When it comes to larger, more complicated projects, that same effect might not kick in quite so readily—even if the designer has invited the homeowner to get involved in the project.

One example of why involving clients in the process is considered such a successful strategy has been so frequently shared that it seems to have nearly attained the level of a scientific *fact*. You've likely encountered a version of the story before: boxed cake mix manufacturers allegedly found that families enjoyed making cakes at home far more when they got to not just stir the mix but also add an egg.[68]

As appealing as that theory is, however, sometimes, *more* can just mean *more work*. Cracking an extra egg or two is relatively easy. Requiring significantly more than that can quickly turn a seemingly simple DIY project into drudgery. And it's worth noting the second half of the IKEA Effect: people don't just value what they've created themselves. They might also take their failures more to heart.[69]

Hiding Better Easter Eggs

Creating enjoyable surprises can be an excellent way to focus a client's attention on the features that their new design offers them—and prevent any less-than-ideal surprises from overwhelming a homeowner.

Pixar's Ed Catmull, for example, has detailed in *Creativity, Inc.*, just how much time (and effort, and teamwork) goes into creating one single movie. In revealing how important it is to the success of Pixar's (undeniably popular and incredibly well-loved) movies that the team pays attention not just to the plot or the characters, but also to the small, sometimes *hidden* details,[70] Catmull provides a useful reminder to designers.

When designing a project, it can be easy to get used to the featured elements and forget just how incredible what you're designing will be for your client. As Sean pointed out, when describing his design that made his client cry tears of joy, *wasn't it just a swimming pool?* To her, however, it was far more than just another pool. And, much like the numerous "hidden," beautiful details that movie studios take care to include in order to surprise and delight their audiences, the seemingly small, surprising details a designer includes in a project can be what amaze a client the most.

Those "Easter eggs," as they're commonly known, rarely go

unnoticed: numerous blogs and websites are dedicated to analyzing even the most minor details and visual surprises in movies and video games. Such details are not limited to popular movies and games. As far back as 1759, Laurence Sterne's novel, *The Life and Opinions of Tristram Shandy, Gentleman,* made full use of the latest technology to incorporate surprises into printed text. He included unusual punctuation—like extra-long dashes, for example—and even printed a solid black page to mark the death of a character.

For designers and builders, therefore, involving clients in the design and build process presents intriguing opportunities. Done right, it can be a very successful strategy. Barry Justus's client, for example, enjoyed the details revealed during the design phase so much that he was willing to expand the project. Shane might include in his final presentation that pillow his clients liked so much online, or Mike might not just start his 3D presentation from inside his client's newly renovated master suite. He might also go one step further and incorporate their new custom desk to surprise them with the view they'll soon see from it. Other designers might trigger a similar client-pleasing effect by inviting clients to get hands-on, teaching them to complete a project that matches their skill level and interests, like planting an herb garden or painting a personalized garden plaque, for example.

Like the visual surprises in Sterne's novel, the "Easter eggs" that delight moviegoers as much as homeowners aren't just there to be cataloged. That solid black page didn't just stand as proof of concept. It added meaning to the story. Sterne, like Catmull, and like Barry Justus and Sean O'Neil, used the latest technology to improve and develop his story—charming the audience while demonstrating remarkable skill.

Key Takeaways

For many homeowners, design plans can seem like optical illusions—and it's only when you help them see the "trick" behind the illusion that they can understand the true merit of your plans.

- Prove your expertise by addressing your client's needs in a form that the client can easily understand, like a 3D rendering or a story.
- Offer options thoughtfully to avoid overwhelming clients with too many choices.
- Get homeowners invested by getting them involved:
  - Hide "Easter eggs" for them to discover as they explore your design.
  - Teach them to complete a small project—like planting an herb garden—that they can claim as "theirs" in the finished project.

FOUR

DESIGN IN 3D—
AND IN PHASES

The question is not what you look at,
but what you see.
—Henry David Thoreau[71]

IF YOU WERE TO ASK someone to name the world's most famous painting, their answer would likely echo the top online search results: the *Mona Lisa* or *Starry Night*. Both paintings have been admired, studied, remixed, and reproduced for so long—and in such mind-boggling quantities—that Leonardo da Vinci and Vincent Van Gogh have attained near-mythic status. From coffee mugs to convincing forgeries, catchy pop songs to learned scholarly tomes—*Mona Lisa*'s "enigmatic" smile and *Starry Night*'s deep blue swirls have gone beyond mere popularity to become iconic.

So popular is the *Mona Lisa*, in fact, that she—for such is the painting's fame that the work is often referred to as she, not it—is visited by six million people annually in her very own multimillion-dollar exhibition space. Behind bulletproof glass, lit by tinted spotlights—and, rumor has it, with her own mailbox to receive the stream of love letters sent by admirers—the *Mona Lisa* is more than just another painting. She has become as well-known as Leonardo himself.

Her fame is such that even a forgery was offered up for

73

thousands.[72] That number, of course, pales in comparison to the recent sale of a painting that even experts could not fully agree really was done by Leonardo da Vinci: $450.3 million.[73]

As well-loved as these popular paintings are, another painting might, according to art historians, actually win the honor of being named the most significant. The reason is hinted at in the answer to a trick question, one favored by teachers introducing students to poetry books and art exhibits. How many poems does a book contain? How many paintings are on an exhibit's walls?

In response, eager students will turn to a book's table of contents to start counting. That number, however, is just a starting point. The trick, of course, is that the collection itself can stand as a poem, too, adding one more number to that carefully counted list.[74]

The most famous painting, therefore, might not be one anyone would recognize at all—if it still existed. Like that one extra poem hidden in plain sight, the most significant painting of all might be the one that had a tremendous impact on art—and design, and architecture—as we know it today, even though the painting itself hasn't been accounted for in more than 500 years: Filippo Brunelleschi's (re)discovery of linear perspective in 1415 with his painting of the baptistery in Florence.[75]

The Scale Model That Stood for 50 Years

In the early 1400s, Filippo Brunelleschi was facing a quandary that is likely still familiar to designers and builders today: how to complete a project that had been delayed time and again.

Beautiful plans for the new cathedral of Santa Maria del Fiore in Florence had been created, but the chosen plans had turned out to be a bit too innovative: no one quite knew how to build the envisioned dome. A model of the dome had been developed in the late thirteenth century, but after fifty years, construction of the dome hadn't really progressed beyond that first model. The dome—intended to be the largest since the Roman era—had instead become a decades-long conundrum. To Brunelleschi's contemporaries, the dome seemed impossible to determine how to build. That no one could quite agree on how to build the dome, however, did not stop construction of the cathedral.[76]

Even as construction continued, the dome remained a challenge. Not building it, however, was not an option. Not only was the model of it kept on display, but the artists, architects, and guilds of the city also produced a truly remarkable number of letters and documents in discussing how the cathedral was to be built, many of which still exist today.[77]

That model on display was on a rather grander scale than the small wax models Michelangelo later created for his clients, but it served a similar purpose: to provide proof of concept and to earn the support of the client. And while fifteenth-century Florence didn't yet have social media to keep interested locals informed of developments, the city didn't need it. Building that magnificent dome exactly as planned had become a goal that seemingly everyone in Florence was eager to achieve—just as building Paul's project exactly as they'd shown it to their friends on Facebook had become a matter of personal fulfillment for Jason and Jennifer.

In the fifteenth century, architects frequently built remarkably detailed and immersive models for clients to explore and examine. Much like the 3D plans that designers today invite clients to "walk" through, the plans that architects then created were sometimes so large and so detailed that clients could literally walk through them.[78] As grand as the model of the dome was, others were sometimes even larger. Those "scale" models, however, were often more decorative than they were mathematically precise.[79]

The person who would eventually figure out how to build the enormous dome took a rather different approach than any of the architects who had come before him. In fact, he wasn't originally an architect at all. Filippo Brunelleschi was a goldsmith and a clockmaker[80] who had begun to earn a reputation for his inventions but who had also, along the way, begun to earn something of a reputation as more than just an inventive thinker. According to his biographer, Giorgio Vasari, Brunelleschi was not exactly known as a calm, mild-mannered type: he sometimes grew so "heated" as he tried to explain his plans that his audience "believed in him less and less, and held him to be an ass and a babbler." His behavior was such that he was kicked out of at least one meeting: "the greater grew their doubts about his proposal," until, at last, "he was carried away bodily from the audience by their servants, being thought to be wholly mad."[81]

Brunelleschi took that treatment to heart, according to his biographer: "this affront was the reason that Filippo could afterwards say that he did not dare to pass through any part of the city, for fear lest someone might say: 'There goes that madman.'"[82] He was certainly becoming recognizable; however, he was earning that recognition not just for his art but also for his personality.

The very project that helped earn Brunelleschi so much attention might have also given rise to some concern that his extraordinary plans for the dome were nothing more than the "babbl[ing]" of a "madman:" the research he undertook with his friend Donatello in Rome.

Silver Mirrors and Video Game Ceilings: Experiencing the World in 3D

In the six hundred years that have passed since Brunelleschi devised both his famous lost painting and his plans for the dome of the cathedral that still stands in Florence today, both linear perspective and 3D scale models have become so familiar as to even seem routine.

At the time, however, both were extraordinary. Whether or not that lost painting was truly the first to employ linear perspective, its popularity and influence were such that, even centuries later, Brunelleschi is still known as the "inventor" of linear perspective. Today, you can still stand where Brunelleschi once stood and see the baptistery; very little has changed from when he stood there.

His painting was startlingly immersive as well as technologically intriguing. Even the trick to seeing it was innovative: instead of standing in front of the painting, a viewer would stand behind the painting, holding it up to their face with one hand to look through the small peephole drilled into it. Through the peephole, the viewer would see the painting reflected in a mirror held in their other hand. Brunelleschi even accounted for varying weather conditions by using silver to reflect the actual sky instead of painting it.[83]

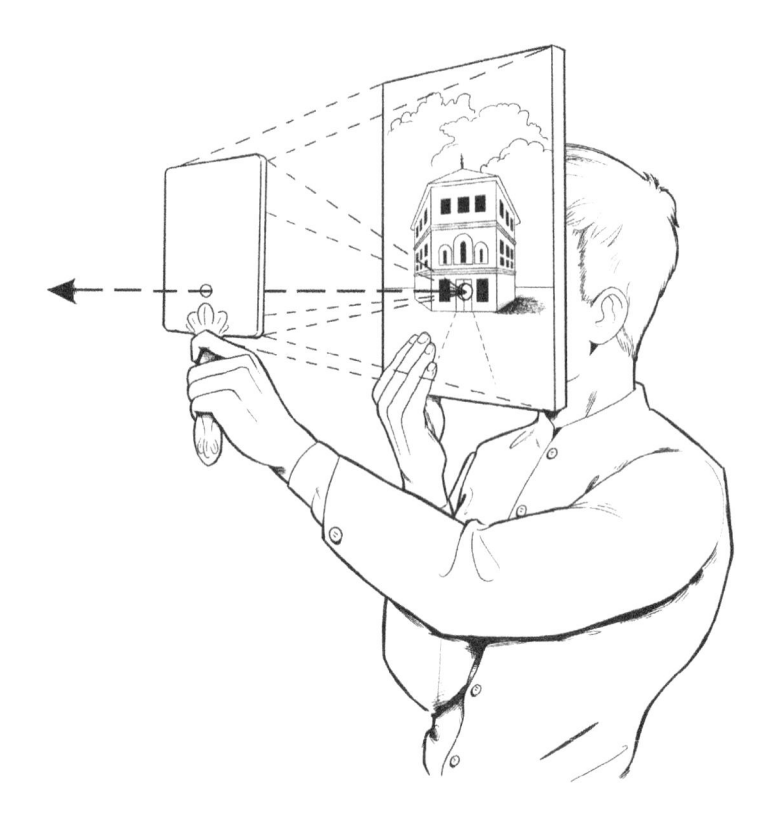

To create that painting, Brunelleschi built on his studies of Roman antiquities. He, along with his friend, the sculptor Donatello, had spent years studying ancient Roman ruins. While his studies with Donatello helped him develop the ideas that would lead to his famous, transformative painting, the enthusiasm with which he approached the ruins he was studying also led people to question his character: he looked sometimes "like a man out of his mind." Not only did he and Donatello carefully measure what they could see, but they also sometimes dug out around the ruins to better understand how the structures had been built.[84] The painting he achieved, after those years of surveying, therefore, was as much math as it was art. He painted exactly what he could see, using geometry to include the building and its environs:

DESIGN IN 3D—AND IN PHASES

> *He gave much attention to perspective, which was then in a very evil plight by reason of many errors that were made therein; and in this he spent much time, until he found by himself a method whereby it might become true and perfect—namely, that of tracing it with the ground-plan and profile and by means of intersecting lines, which was something truly most ingenious and useful to the art of design. In this he took so great delight that he drew with his own hand the Piazza di S. Giovanni, with all the compartments of black and white marble wherewith that church was incrusted, which he foreshortened with singular grace; and he drew, likewise, the building of the Misericordia, with the shops of the Wafer-Makers and the Volta de' Pecori, and the column of S. Zanobi on the other side.*[85]

Brunelleschi's precision was remarkable. While his contemporaries might have grown accustomed to being able to wander around inside of one of the grand scale models, his audience also understood that the model they explored would likely (or even inevitably) differ from the finished product. In fact, the vetting process for the dome proposal was as lengthy and competitive as it was in part because buildings sometimes collapsed unexpectedly—a fate that the cathedral committee obviously wished to avoid.[86]

With his painting, Brunelleschi suggested that models and plans could be so precise that they didn't just hint at what could be—they truly mirrored reality. He didn't have photographs or videos or virtual reality or augmented reality. What he had, instead, was a painting, a peephole, and a mirror. When all three were brought together, viewers could enter an entirely new world that looked exactly like the real world before them. It's not entirely surprising that viewers of Brunelleschi's painting were unable to quite tell whether they were looking at the real world or a painting through that peephole—his technique was so new that it would very quickly inspire an entire generation of painters, who would go on to shape what we now recognize as art in the West.

Before Brunelleschi and other revolutionary Renaissance artists began to reimagine Florence, the city was not quite as beautiful as it stands today. He and his fellow Renaissance artists transformed the city, using art and design, sketches and scale models, painting and architecture. In inviting the viewer to look through that tiny drilled hole, Brunelleschi also invited the viewer to stand where he did and see what he had seen. In so doing, he put the viewer right at the center.

Until Renaissance artists popularized linear perspective, the placement of things like ceilings, floors, and thrones in paintings often seemed a bit untethered to reality. Today, people are so accustomed to being right at the center of what they're viewing that even free video games[87] make it effortlessly easy to place oneself right in the center of one's own constructed reality—to adjust the character to suit one's own appearance, or even to change details like the height of the ceiling or the size of the furniture until it feels familiar to the viewer (or game player).

Linear perspective and 3D drawings make it easy to imagine that one is seeing more than just a sketch of an idea; instead, the viewer is right in the center of the drawing, seeing the world as it is—or as it could be.

From $15K to $150K: Designing in Phases

Although the construction of Brunelleschi's dome began six hundred years ago, its design process and its construction challenges would be remarkably familiar to designers today. From tight housing arrangements to frequent committee meetings, designer Barry Justus and his crew might have found the conditions under which that fifteenth-century crew began to build the dome remarkably similar to those under which they built the pool on the cliff. Just as Barry's crew faced a 130-ft drop into the frozen lake below, the crew building the dome kicked off their work—at long last—one hundred forty feet up.[88] Just as Justus had to arrange catering for his own crew, so too did Brunelleschi need to figure out a way to get meals to workers perched high above the city. It was, his biographer acknowledges, "a very great inconvenience for anyone who had climbed to the top to descend to the ground, and the builders lost much time in going to eat and drink, and suffered great discomfort in the heat of the day."[89] His solution: "Filippo therefore made arrangements for eating-houses with kitchens to be opened on the cupola, and for wine to be sold there, so that no one had to leave his [labor] until the evening, which was convenient for the men and very advantageous for the work."[90]

It's no wonder Brunelleschi needed to make such arrangements for his crew: the cathedral ultimately took a long list of builders centuries to complete. From the time the foundation stone was placed to the time Michelangelo was asked his opinion of the as yet unfinished drum of the dome, nearly two hundred years had passed.

As Brunelleschi's dome proves, planning and building projects in phases can be a remarkably successful strategy: it still stands today, as impressive in the twenty-first century as it was in the fifteenth. Of course, not every project is quite as massive—or as time-consuming—as Brunelleschi's dome. Regardless of the size of the project, however, after planning the perfect design and planning the perfect story...the next step is to bring both together.

Jesse, a designer in Phoenix, Arizona who specialized in innovative swimming pool designs, found a way to bring the perfect story and the perfect design together in ways his client, like Brunelleschi's viewers, didn't imagine possible. Not only was

Jesse's client Ken surprised to find that Jesse was ready to discuss with him what he would like to do with his project, but he was later also amazed at just how easily Jesse showed him multiple options for a space that had been deemed hopeless.

To Jesse, who was accustomed to offering his clients innovative designs, the surprise that day was not a "hopeless" space. It was that no one else had managed to offer Ken what he really wanted.

As he drove to meet Ken, Jesse expected to find himself designing in a rather small, cramped backyard. He had fit Ken into a last-minute opening in his schedule, so he had not had the time to research the property before their appointment. When he arrived, he was surprised to find that the client lived on a large, unfinished property. Given what Ken had asked for—just a small outdoor kitchen, on a budget of $15K—he would have expected to find a significantly smaller space, perhaps one with pre-existing landscaping or hardscaping he would need to take into account when designing the new kitchen.

With so much space available, it was surprising to Jesse that the client wanted nothing more than a small kitchen. The house was beautiful, the lawn spacious, and the client affable. As they chatted, Jesse decided to ask if Ken had been thinking about doing anything with the rest of his property, because, even as unfinished as it was, Jesse thought it seemed like a really beautiful space for Ken and his family to enjoy.

"I don't know," Ken answered, shrugging. "Maybe one day we'll put in a pool or something. We're not going to worry about that now. We really just want the kitchen. I love to barbecue, so that's what we're going to do."

That afternoon, Jesse learned a lot about his client. As they walked the property together, they chatted about everything from how he liked his barbecue to how he and his family liked to spend their time. Jesse noted details that would help him make sure the kitchen he designed for them would be just right. Even though the client was asking for a relatively small project, Jesse knew from experience that his clients typically loved the extra, personalized details that he always included in his design presentations. He wanted to include some of those extra-special details for Ken and his family, too.

Designing the Project

Back in his office, Jesse thought about what Ken had said. The words "maybe one day" served as a source of inspiration, and Jesse—who had been able to see potential in Ken's yard even before gathering information from Ken—felt up to the challenge. After designing an outdoor kitchen ideal for grilling, Jesse started to plan additional features he thought they'd enjoy. A fire pit was the first "extra" option to be added. It took no time at all to incorporate one into his 3D design—and it was affordable enough that it wouldn't require much stretching of that $15K budget at all.

The client had mentioned a pool, too, so Jesse set to work designing a pool that would make the most of that spacious and inviting yard. The family enjoyed spending time together, but their empty yard made them feel disconnected, so Jesse arranged the kitchen, lounge area, swimming pool, and landscaping to fit seamlessly together, each area connecting invitingly to the next. So that the family could continue to enjoy each area as it was built, he also made sure each piece of his design would be easy to build in phases, whenever the client was ready to expand beyond the outdoor kitchen he wanted in time for his next barbecue.

Presenting the Project

At their next meeting, Jesse began by sharing just his plans for the outdoor kitchen—much to the client's delight. He had given Ken exactly what he'd wanted: a kitchen perfect for grilling. Jesse did not stop there, however. He then introduced the next phase of his presentation by saying, "I was really excited by your yard, and I was thinking about what you said. Since you said you were thinking about adding a swimming pool one day, let me show you what we can do."

With that, he presented his client with the rest of his design, following up on that outdoor kitchen with a new swimming pool plus full landscaping. The client was so delighted that he signed on the spot. That $15K outdoor kitchen had turned into a $150K project.

Signing the Contract

As Jesse and Ken chatted about the plans, Ken told Jesse that he was far from the first designer he'd called. He was, however, the first who'd understood what Ken really wanted—and then given it to him, in incredible detail.

Ken's underlying concern—the reason he'd at first waved off the question of what else he wanted to do with his yard—was not the budget. It was that he'd been let down one too many times before. Like Brunelleschi's clients, who worried that his plans were too ambitious and the dome would collapse, Ken was hesitant to ask yet another designer to attempt such a big project when he'd called for so many estimates, sat through so many brief presentations, and never—before Jesse's arrival—met with anyone who'd been able to help him visualize what he really wanted.

Ken was especially delighted by Jesse's design because he hadn't expected a designer to take the initiative and offer even more than he'd asked for. After being disappointed by the limited options other estimates had offered, Ken had broken down the project into increasingly smaller pieces. By the time he called

Jesse, he had decided to ask for nothing more than a small outdoor kitchen.

Unlike Jesse, the handful of designers whom Ken had called for estimates hadn't even hinted that more could be done, even after seeing his wide-open property. They had just said, "Great! We'll get that kitchen done for you!" The sketches they had offered, however, hadn't measured up to what he really wanted. Ken, after all, didn't want just a solitary outdoor kitchen. What he wanted was something worth his investment. Jesse, like Brunelleschi six hundred years before, achieved the seemingly impossible by completely reimagining the entire project.

It hadn't taken Jesse much extra work or extra time. But by listening to what the client really wanted, seeing the potential in his space, and helping his client visualize what would be possible, he earned a project worth 10x what he'd originally expected: instead of just spending $15K on a small outdoor kitchen, Jesse's client renovated his entire outdoor living space for $150K.

Four-Packs of Beer:
Why Designing in Phases Works

Jesse's strategy is backed up by research: people really like things that are framed together as a set. Researchers studying how "completeness" affects the decision-making process found that offering items framed in orderly, easily understood sets can be remarkably motivating.[91]

Their results suggest an unintended consequence of not considering the importance of framing when offering a client options. When offered beer to purchase, the participants in one research study typically opted to buy six beers. That number is so readily linked to beer, after all, that a "six-pack" is commonly understood to mean *beer*. Given a container, however, the participants in Barasz's study filled it - and bought only four instead of six when given a package with just four slots.

As Jesse understood, offering a new package can produce completely different results. Had he just offered his client that beautiful outdoor kitchen, he would likely still have earned the contract. Ken did, after all, really love the kitchen Jesse had designed. By reframing, Jesse didn't just expand the project—he absolutely delighted his client.

The reason Jesse's approach was so successful has as much to do with his listening skills as his technical design skills. He took the time to understand what it was his client was really saying during that first appointment. As Ken chatted about the meal he was looking forward to making for his family, Jesse heard the details in the story that he would build on to give Ken and his family a space they could all enjoy together.

> **Characters:** A warm, friendly family with young kids.
>
> **Plot:** That warm and friendly family wants to connect more with their friends and neighbors, so they want a welcoming outdoor space that they can use throughout the year.

Jesse started with an outdoor kitchen that would be ideal for summer barbecues. Then, he added a fire pit where everyone could relax and hang out while the food cooked. There was plenty of room for the pool that Ken had admitted to considering for the future, so Jesse designed a pool, too—one that the kids would love to play in. He situated that kid-friendly pool within easy sight of the outdoor kitchen so that Ken would be able to keep an eye on his kids while he grilled.

As he walked Ken through his design plans, Jesse began to

tell that story, explaining how the new options fit together. He didn't just point out that he'd added a fire pit. He incorporated it into the story that he was shaping, helping his client see why it would be a great addition: with the fire pit, Ken wouldn't be alone out there in a big, empty yard while he was grilling in his new outdoor kitchen. The fire pit had been placed in a great spot for Ken's family and friends to hang out while they waited for dinner—and to whet their appetite for the enticing meal he was preparing.

Phase One: The outdoor kitchen, ideal for summer barbecues.

Phase Two: The new lounge area, perfect for friends and family to hang out while Ken grilled.

Phase Three: The new pool, situated so that Ken could keep an eye on the kids while grilling and while relaxing with guests in the new lounge area.

Jesse hadn't expected Ken to do all three phases at once. To help his client see the value in designing in phases, he pointed out how each phase worked with the prior one as he went over the options—demonstrating not just how he'd make sure each phase complemented the others, if Ken were to decide he wanted to add on in the future, but also how he'd make sure that construction for each new phase would minimally impact the completed areas of the project.

Ken, however, was so thrilled with the results that he was ready to start construction on the entire project immediately.

The Egg on the Table: Getting Clients Ready to Sign

It's the rare masterpiece that is completed in just one sitting. While both Pablo Picasso and Salvador Dalí, it seems, hit upon one expedient way to turn even the mundane act of paying bills into art—Picasso seems to have realized recipients might value his signature on a check more than the promise of payment,[92] and Dalí is said to have noticed the same would happen if he dashed off a sketch on a check—both typically spent a bit more time on their work than just a quick signature or hasty sketch required.

Such art did not always need to take a great deal of time, however. In 1949, for example, Picasso very quickly created art that was far more recognizable as such than just a simple signature. He and photographer Gjon Mili created "light paintings" together. Holding a lightbulb instead of a paintbrush, Picasso drew in the air as Mili photographed him. His lightbulb drawings took just milliseconds to create, but the results were preserved in Mili's photographs.[93]

Fascinating as those light paintings are, they are not widely ranked among Picasso's masterpieces. *Guernica*, created for the 1937 World Fair, is today known as one of his most significant paintings. It was painted in a matter of weeks[94]—a relatively short amount of time when compared with the *Mona Lisa*, the world's most recognizable and valuable painting, which took Leonardo da Vinci four years to complete.[95]

Brunelleschi's dome, and the cathedral it was designed for, took centuries to complete. And while today the dome of the cathedral in Florence is known as Brunelleschi's dome, names even more well-known today than Brunelleschi's also gave their input into the dome, including Donatello, Leonardo da Vinci, and even Michelangelo.

Donatello was not just one of Brunelleschi's close friends. The two, after all, had studied Roman architecture together, surveying the ruins in the years before he eventually won the commission to build the dome.[96] Leonardo da Vinci was an apprentice in Andrea del Verrocchio's studio when Verrocchio helped position the bronze ball at the top of the dome. And in a story that might be apocryphal, Michelangelo is said to have offended the man tasked with completing the drum of the dome after Brunelleschi's death, Baccio D'Agnolo, by comparing it to a "cricket cage."[97]

That it took such an incredible team to build a structure that has stood for so many centuries is a testament to its grandeur. To earn such an extraordinary commission, Brunelleschi did not rely on his impressive design skills alone. He knew that his plans would work—but he, like Jesse and Michelangelo and Barry Justus, needed to find a way to prove that to the client.

The model that he created for the dome competition was impressively large and incredibly detailed—but, detailed as it was, it alone did not earn him the job. After all, as gorgeous as models at the time often were, buildings built from those models still sometimes collapsed. In order to prove that he could build what he promised, Brunelleschi turned to a far simpler and far more familiar model: an egg.

When explaining his plans, Brunelleschi did not go into detail as to how his unusual model technically worked. Instead, he decided to show them: he made an egg stand on a table by gently cracking its base.[98] He understood that being able to *see* was often more inspiring than just hearing how results would be achieved.

A project does not need to take quite as long as Brunelleschi's dome—or involve quite as many designers, architects, and artisans—to be successfully completed in stages. Like Brunelleschi—and like Barry Justus, when creating those new plans for the pool on the cliff—Jesse understood what some of his fellow designers did not: that showing a client a vision of what is possible can be tremendously motivating.

Of course, pool builders and landscape designers are limited by certain physical constraints. Unlike Brunelleschi and his contemporaries, who would build large-scale models that clients could literally walk inside, designers today cannot literally take clients "inside" a planned project. What they can do, instead, is create an interactive 3D design that clients can "walk" through—and, in the process, they can include just as much detail as the finished project itself.

Pool buyers, after all, can't test drive a pool the same way they can test drive a car. But just as car dealers invite buyers to not just look at a car but also to hop in and take it for a drive themselves, designers can invite clients to experience "reality" in completely new and absolutely thrilling ways by not just offering an interactive 3D model to explore, and not just planning a story to share, but also by creating a fully realized experience, personalized for the client.

Key Takeaways

When Filippo Brunelleschi (re)discovered linear perspective in the early 1400s, he transformed art as we know it. By applying to painting what he'd learned studying the ruins of Roman architecture, he paved the way for the designers, builders, architects, and artists of today.

- Make presentations easy for clients to understand. Take a cue from Brunelleschi, who left out the technical details and memorably cracked an egg to show how his dome would stand.
- Show clients how to complete a project in phases. Their outdoor living space won't take as long as a cathedral, but their kids might feel like it does. Explaining the phases helps them feel involved.
- Place your client at the center. Since Brunelleschi, viewers have gotten used to art that mirrors reality. Mirror theirs with anchoring details:
    - Draw their house in 3D.
    - Personalize the details: show them their kitchen curtains from the deck or their new car in the driveway.
    - Add scale figures to show the size of the project, like swimmers in the pool.

FIVE

SURPRISE YOUR CLIENTS

The best thing of the present day is that every discovery...
tends to bring everything within reach of the common people.
—Thomas Edison[99]

IN THE YEAR 2000, IN a conference room full of executives in Arizona, I presented the first real-time, interactive 3D pool design to a team of pool builders.

At the time, 3D technology was not yet readily accessible. Real-time 3D was fairly new even to video games. Computer scientists in university labs had been steadily improving 3D graphics for decades, but the programs that existed were not just expensive—they also often required extensive training, if not an advanced degree. The work done by scientists like Ivan Sutherland and others at schools like MIT had inspired generations of students, artists, and developers to think about fascinating new ways to bring 3D beyond the computer screen and into the real world—but the technology that existed still hadn't quite made it into the hands of pool builders.

Counted among those inspired by early innovators like Sutherland? Me, for one—plus the artists and developers like Patrick Smith who joined me in making that very first interactive 3D pool design happen. Getting interactive 3D design into the hands of designers and builders was our goal—and to get it there, we needed to test the idea in front of some potential users.

When the opportunity arose to present the software that would become known as Pool Studio to the executives at Paddock Pools in Phoenix, Arizona, I hopped on a plane.

At the time, Paddock Pools was the second-largest pool company in the world—and Buzz Ghiz was not one to just rest on the laurels they'd earned. He was aiming at a new multimillion-dollar home builder account, and, when he heard about my experimental 3D pool from Joe Vassallo, his sales manager, he saw the potential: a custom 3D design was what he was looking for to set his company apart.

No laptop was powerful enough at the time to run the software, so I packed up my desktop tower and loaded it into the plane's overhead compartment. As I mentally reviewed my presentation during the flight, I wondered whether experienced executives would react to seeing ideas in 3D with quite the same enthusiasm as my fellow students had.

Just months prior—in a move that probably foreshadowed my later decision to skip college in favor of developing Pool Studio—I had skipped the suggested route to solving a homework networking assignment and instead mapped out the three-story building network in 3D. It had been a personal challenge: I had wanted to see just how intricate and detailed I could make it.

The response was incredible. The professor was so impressed by the presentation that, even though I had made a couple of mistakes in my network layout, I still managed to earn the highest grade in that class. Only when I saw my fellow students' reactions to the 3D design did I realize that I'd hit on something more than just a neat way to earn a better grade. Sharing ideas in 3D, it turned out, was far more than just a powerful visualization tool. It was also an incredibly helpful way to share ideas that were hard to explain in 2D drawings—or even just words. Whether Buzz and the pool builders would love it, too, however, remained to be seen.

Like a lot of other college-age kids studying computer networking immediately following the era of Y2K (the acronym given to the Year 2000 Problem, which had posited that computer dates ticking over from "99" to "00" in the new year would potentially cause widespread mayhem), I had absorbed at least one lesson from that highly debated event: how a question was presented could often become just as significant as the question itself—and the answers.

The executives assembled in that conference room were analyzing a question faced by many builders: how to sell more pools in less time. How to actually do that was the subject of considerable discussion.

I identified one common issue: homeowners often couldn't quite see how the promising ideas offered were actually going to get built. For every charismatic designer who could sell an enthralled family on little more than a hasty sketch on the back of a napkin, there were far more who struggled to share detailed plans in terms clients fully grasped.

A new pool or an updated landscape or a complete backyard renovation is rarely a project undertaken casually, after all. Given how significant of an investment such a project often is, homeowners understandably want to be sure they understand everything going on. Whether it's terminology (what exactly is *gunite* again?) or scale (just how much space will the deck take up relative to the pool?), explaining the details can turn out to be a rather time-consuming task.

For clients with flat lawns and maybe even some "builder's special" hardscaping already in place to provide some context, that process might be relatively straightforward. For clients like Barry's—trying to figure out how to build a pool on a cliff overlooking a lake when there was still ten feet of snow on the ground—it would be far more complicated.

In that Arizona conference room, the executives reacted to the sight of that first 3D pool design exactly as the students exploring my 3D network map had: they were blown away. In fact, that 3D pool design—presented on a screen hooked up to my desktop computer, which had less computing power than today's smartphones—earned a startled "Wow!" from more than one member of the audience.

That it would be possible, within less than 20 years, to take that 3D pool design from a screen in a conference room or a laptop on the homeowner's kitchen table and instead share it as a professional-quality interactive 360° video on social media—or even create an augmented reality design on the spot, while walking around the homeowner's yard with just a tablet in hand—would probably have triggered even more exclamations of surprise.

In 2000, social media networks barely existed. Mobile phones looked more like plastic television remote controls than today's sleek glass smartphones. The battery life of those plastic phones might have been enviable, but the screens often seemed scarcely any bigger than a postage stamp—and were about as visually compelling as a sheet out of a dot-matrix printer. The only tablets that would have looked familiar then were PDAs—personal digital assistants. Those PDAs did have touchscreens—if rather pixelated, grayscale ones—but it would be some time before those screens would be ready for a designer to create and share a complete design right on the spot.

The executives in that conference room were not new to pool design. They were experienced professionals, familiar with the latest advances in the industry—and yet even they were surprised by just how exciting it was to see that first pool in not only 3D but also *interactive* 3D. To be able to explore the pool from any angle—including underwater—was frankly incredible, even for the seasoned builders who had been in the industry for years.

Telling the story to unveil that unprecedented 3D pool took just a few minutes. Readying the technology to share it, however, was the work of many years—maybe even six centuries' worth.

Because for designers imagining innovative pools as much as for Brunelleschi engineering that dome in Florence, earning the opportunity to build something original has always taken more than just an innovative idea or even a perfect plan. The idea, the technology, the story: all need to come together to truly surprise and delight the client.

From "To Be or Not To Be" to Whodunit: Surprises Make the Story

In many of the most memorable stories, a good twist is crucial. Leo Tolstoy probably could have told a pretty good story about a pretty happy family. Agatha Christie likely could have written a relaxing story about friendly vacationers enjoying a few days on a private island. Both, however, understood that a recitation of even the nicest facts could turn a good story into a boring one.

Readers don't stay up late with a dry, boring novel any more than fans hover at the edge of their seats—ready to leap up and join in the cheering—for a predictable game. Fans don jerseys, glued to the action, not only because they want to see what's going to happen next (Are they really going to make that Hail Mary pass? Will the rookie really score a goal in his very first game?) but also because they want to feel like they're a part of the action.

Building anticipation can take different routes that all lead up to that game-changing moment. When it works, the results are unmistakable. Maybe success comes when the arena is wildly cheering that a hockey team broke its nearly fifty-year struggle to win another championship. Or maybe it's when Sean's client signed the contract after she burst into tears of joy at the sight of her dream yard. Or maybe it's when Jesse's ability to plan a project in phases led his client to shake his hand and sign on the spot for a project worth 10x the original budget.

These stories all unfolded differently—in each case, however, the unfolding story achieved what Robert McKee, in his classic study of storytelling, has identified as crucial: each story connected with the audience both emotionally and intellectually. And as McKee proves in his analysis of how stories really work, the surprise can be a subtle one.[100] What matters is that the story doesn't just snag the audience's attention—it keeps it.

Anyone familiar with sharing 3D designs with clients, for example, might have nodded along knowingly as Sean began to realize why his client burst into tears. Mystery novel fans would have recognized—as Jesse did—that his client's comment to not worry about the rest of the yard just yet hinted that there was more to his story than had been revealed.

In the familiar form of a five-act story, the twist often arrives right in the structural middle, in the climactic third act. The surprise is revealed, the revelation changes the game, and the characters face crucial decisions. That twist doesn't have to be on the scale of an Agatha Christie mystery or an enormous Russian novel. In fact, sometimes the twist itself turns out to be less important than the fact that a twist exists.

Researchers studying communication strategies have found that memory can be fickle—sometimes, not only do people forget crucial details but they also forget which one of the pieces of information they heard was actually important. Sometimes—in a quirk of communication tactics occasionally exploited by advertisements and political campaigns—just mentioning an idea can cause a "sleeper effect" that will make an idea even more persuasive later on, when the original context has been forgotten.[101]

That's one reason a cliffhanger's mere existence can be more memorable than its resolution. Diehard fans might remember exactly what each and every player on the team was doing as the clock ran out and the quarterback launched a Hail Mary pass. Mystery buffs might analyze each and every twist and turn of a riveting novel to spot the clues leading up to the reveal. But sometimes the fact that there was a cliffhanger at all is what really makes an impact.

The popular television show *Dallas*, for example, ended one season with an unexpected shooting so startling that discussion of who shot the main character went far beyond water-cooler small talk. It even became a talking point between political parties during the 1980 presidential election.

We remember there was a twist—*Who shot JR?*—but few today remember the answer as readily, let alone the reasons driving the cliffhanger, even though the episode revealing the answer earned an enormous audience of more than eighty million.[102] The question itself has entered the lexicon.

Now, it's no longer a surprise when a television series ends a season with a suspenseful cliffhanger. And developing a so-called hook to pull readers into an article is such a time-honored tradition that even the most junior writer on a college paper can typically spin a story about the obstacles any given star of any given team had to overcome in order to achieve success. Creating a surprising story that is genuinely unexpected, however, takes careful planning.

Novelists like Charles Dickens figured out one way to keep readers coming back for more. His stories were serialized, appearing in relatively short installments that were full of enough startling revelations, unexpected arrivals, and seemingly insurmountable obstacles to keep enough readers riveted that publication remained profitable. Storytellers like Dickens have long used the structure of their chosen format to heighten interest and build suspense. That strategy works equally well whether writing a novel of considerable length or trying your hand at a three-line haiku.

When the three-volume novel was popular, for example,

writers would structure—and restructure—their stories to fit that preferred format. Even Mary Shelley, whose novel *Frankenstein* has remained popular for two hundred years, edited her story into (and out of) the three-volume format to suit her tale—and her audience. When it's an outdoor renovation rather than a television show or novel, however, there isn't quite the same call for 32-page installments or a mustache-twirling villain (unless it's to use sound effects to demonstrate how the water features and planned landscaping work together to mute the sounds of any particularly noisy, metaphorically mustache-twirling neighbors).

Structuring a presentation to include surprises for a client can do more than just demonstrate how the space can be transformed. Those surprises can be especially memorable and important when the client's current space includes noisy neighbors, complicated terrain, or even just bland, cookie-cutter hardscaping. An interactive presentation makes it easy for the client to see how enjoyable the newly designed space will be: sound effects reveal how the pool and water features provide pleasing background noise, for example. Whether surprising the client by including the family dog in the design or by showing them a 3D presentation in the first place—sometimes, the lead-up to the surprise is what helps to create the most memorable and enjoyable experience, just as Hamlet's well-known musings leading to his fateful decision make the decision itself all the more powerful.

Telling a great story means bringing all of the key elements together—characters and plot right alongside the design and the technology. When all work together, introducing a thoughtful surprise or two along the way will inspire an enthusiastic *Wow*.

Restaurant Menus and Traffic Times: What Makes a Surprise a Good One?

Of course, not every surprise works out, even when the intentions are excellent. The late, legendary copywriter Jane Maas demonstrated this truth when she shared the story of how an airline carrier scandalized some of their frequent fliers' wives in the 1960s. The airline sent friendly notes of thanks to fliers' wives who had seemingly gone on trips with their husbands; those notes, however, exposed more than one secret rendezvous.[103] That airline's attempt at surprising their customers was certainly not a welcome one—it was more like finding a potentially venomous spider lurking in the bananas than to winning the lottery.

Some stories include surprises that are notably happier than others, even if, as in stories that follow the four-part Kishōtenketsu structure, there is a twist that means the happiness achieved is not quite what might have been expected. Will the grieving prince manage to avenge his father's death? Will the local underdog get to live out his dream of playing college football?[104] Advertisers know that the success of a campaign often hinges on the smallest tweaks to even the most familiar stories.

Claude Hopkins titled his classic book *Scientific Advertising* because he didn't simply try out a few options to see what would stick. He rigorously experimented, keeping a close watch on the results so he could determine what was and was not effective. He built his successful campaigns not on gut instinct but instead on his careful analysis of his detailed and accurate tests, results, and records.

Nearly ninety years later, surgeon Atul Gawande's research into how to best improve performance reinforces Hopkins' analysis. Gawande reveals that paying careful attention to the process can lead to sometimes unexpected results. Certainly, he was well aware of the pattern that his own research revealed: some of the most successful performers were those who continued to rely upon the checklists they had carefully created—even when they had a good feeling about what they were doing. As he admits in his book, he didn't really expect the checklist that he had created to make a truly notable difference in his own surgeries. Using his own checklist, however, helped Gawande and his team catch everything from minor errors to potential disasters. He even credits its use in helping him save more lives.[105]

Whether planning a surgery or an ad campaign, one extensive project or the first phase of a multi-phase renovation, taking a step back to look at the process itself—not just focusing on the main event—can reveal important insights. Jesse understood this when he began his presentation for Ken, the client who said he "just" wanted a small kitchen in his big backyard. He didn't leap straight to the fully detailed $150K version of that "small outdoor kitchen." As excited as Jesse was to share his ideas, he planned an approach that would not just reveal a design that suited Ken's lifestyle, it would also suit Ken's personality and communication style.

He gradually worked up to the big reveal, letting Ken take in what he was seeing before introducing each new element and feature. In so doing, Jesse reassured Ken that he was the right guy for the job. He knew that dropping a splashy design in front of Ken would be overwhelming. Some of his clients, Jesse knew, did enjoy the excitement of the "big reveal," as it were, but Jesse recognized that immediately leaping beyond Ken's request for just a kitchen in favor of his much more extensive (and expensive) concept wasn't the best way to earn Ken's trust.

Instead, he built a story around his design, gradually revealing new details and showing how they slotted seamlessly together. Ken, he had learned from their conversations, was an affable guy who loved to grill just as much as his friends loved to eat his delicious meals. By situating Ken at the center of his story, Jesse kept the focus on how each feature and each new area would add to his—and his friends'—enjoyment of the outdoor living space.

The reason that approach was so successful is suggested by Google's analysis of its users' search results: there are times when people just do not want to be surprised. When Google's analysts took a closer look at search data, they noticed an interesting detail: people like to know what to expect. That is why, they suggest, so many people seem to double-check the details online in advance of a trip or a reservation. They will search for menus, verify restaurant hours, or even check how much of a tip might be expected. Finding answers to questions like these, Google's researchers suggest, helps people avoid unpleasant surprises.[106] It would be the rare adventurer, after all, who would prefer that an evening out actually turn into a whodunit lurching from one Dickensian twist to another.

The insights that Google highlights suggest a useful opportunity, as Jesse understood: making it easy to find and understand helpful information does more than just help clients avoid unpleasant surprises. It also helps connect clients to your design by both reassuring them—and delighting them.

Design to Surprise

Before designer Lea Frederick started designing pools, she trained as an engineer. That background has helped her solve some of her clients' most challenging problems. When Lea first meets with her clients, she sometimes learns that they have called her because their sprawling rural properties have proved a little too challenging to tackle without help. What can seem at first glance like a vast blank slate, ready to be transformed, might instead hide an inconveniently located septic system or a significant grade change.

Because so many of her clients—much like Jesse's client Ken—often turn to her after struggling to get their dream project built, Lea takes care to listen attentively to what it is that her clients want most from their outdoor living space. "It's heartbreaking," she says, "to tell a customer that they paid for a plan that they can't do anything with."

That news can come as an unpleasant surprise. To reassure families that the features they really want actually can get built, Lea employs two remarkably effective techniques.

Create "idea books" of photos

Learning what a client likes can be challenging when the appointment is scheduled before the client's house has even been built. To inspire her clients, Lea invites them to explore photos with her. "It helps me get a really good sense of their style," she says, even when it's "something as simple as the color of the water." Then, she uses these details to inspire her 3D design. And since Lea—like Jesse—often creates designs that can easily be built in phases, she also uses photos to help make sure her clients feel confident that the completed project will look seamless.

Lea delights her clients when she incorporates elements from their idea books into her finished designs: "There are things that they like in the photographs that I can pull out and represent in 3D," Lea says. "It's just a matter of choosing the right materials."

Chatting about what they like in photos, she says, helps reassure the homeowner. She'll tell a client, "Let's design it in now, so when we add it in it doesn't look like it's pieced together as separate projects." That process works: "Having them think out of the box just [makes] that project bigger inherently."

Incorporate the clients in the design

Personalizing the space, the color scheme, and the materials is just the beginning. Lea also encourages her clients to imagine how they see themselves enjoying their yard. Asking specific questions—"For example, tell me how many people you see sitting around [a spa or a fire pit], and we'll work from there"—means she can show them how their dream will be realized in her design:

"We did a design for a guy who said, 'I just want to sit in my pool and watch the sunset over the lake,' and I said, 'I can show you that.' So I moved the sun [in the design], and he's sitting in his floatie with a drink in his hand watching the sunset. He couldn't be happier!"

By showing her clients exactly how her designs give them what they want—by making space for six friends around a fire pit or by moving the sun during the presentation to show how beautiful the view will be when floating in the pool with a drink in hand—Lea brings all of the crucial elements together. The idea, the technology, the story, and the presentation: all work together to help clients decide that they're ready to build.

Sometimes, however, it's easy to unintentionally (or even with the best of intentions) skip a few steps along the path to getting a project completed. Instead of following a checklist—like the ones that Gawande identified as key to success—some might instead try to skip a few steps, ready to leap straight from idea to completion and forgetting to take into account just how important it is to earn a client's trust along the way. Just as a teacher who might not see the need to mention all of the seemingly minor steps involved in solving an equation might, in so doing, fail to help struggling students understand exactly what they need to do to solve that equation, a designer who overlooks the important step of engaging their client's interest and attention can delay or even doom a project.

Aaron discovered just how vital it could be to manage even the seemingly minor or mundane details of a presentation when he decided to try a tip he'd read about: using line drawings to entertain a client's children. He was designing a new pool for Jacob and Natalie, a friendly couple whose kindergartner had very much wanted to be involved in the discussion during their first meeting. Liam—the clients' five year old—had expressed opinions about everything from the depth of the pool ("really deep!") to the color ("really blue!"). That discussion had been entertaining—but also distracting for Jacob and Natalie, whose attention had been a bit divided.

As he was getting ready to head out to present his design, Aaron remembered reading about a new use for one of the lesser-known features offered by design software: line drawings. Aaron had never created a line drawing of a design before—his clients, after all, wanted to see all of the details, rendered as vividly as possible. He remembered reading, however, that the line drawings that design software could automatically generate were strikingly similar to pages from a coloring book. Before he left for Jacob and Natalie's, he selected a handful of quick images, including that big blue pool Liam wanted so badly. He threw in a couple of extras, too, like a great screenshot of the view the client would see when standing in their backyard, facing not just their new pool but also their beloved dream home, which they'd just recently completed. Then he generated the line drawings, printed the sheets, and brought them along for Liam to color.

During the meeting, Aaron didn't think about those line drawings very much, but he noticed that the tip had worked: the line drawings kept Liam happily occupied. While he was busy with his coloring pages, his parents were able to focus on the design itself. Printing out those extra sheets didn't take Aaron much time at all—he'd done it, just before heading out the door. The impact, however, was significant. Just one week later, Aaron learned why they'd chosen his design: Jacob and Natalie had put

Liam's coloring pages up on the fridge and grown attached to their kindergartner's take on just how awesome their backyard was going to be.

It doesn't always require the musings of a Hamlet to persuade a client or an audience. Sometimes, surprising a client in the most memorable way can add only a few extra minutes to the design process. Even seemingly small gestures—like Aaron's printing of those coloring pages to occupy a child's attention, like Brunelleschi's crushing of the tip of an egg to demonstrate how it could stand on a table, or like Lea Frederick's moving of the sun during her presentation to show the client the sky as he was going to experience it in his pool—can be incredibly persuasive.

How to Create a Memorable Surprise

When Jacob and Natalie added Liam's artwork to their fridge, it didn't matter to them that the results were not quite as flawless as they would have been if Aaron had handed them a beautifully printed full-color version to display instead. Their son hadn't quite mastered the art of coloring inside the lines or even of choosing colors that bore at least some resemblance to nature. That big blue pool he'd asked for had become electric purple in his rendition. Liam had added his own touch—both in the cheerful colors he'd picked and especially in the stick figure family that he'd added.

For Jacob and Natalie, their son's artwork was the deciding factor. Sure, they'd considered quite a few other proposals that would have been more than good enough. What they appreciated most, however, was that Aaron had taken the time to thoughtfully include their son in the process. The artwork on the fridge—as whimsically colorful as it was—represented what they really wanted: for their growing family to have an inviting place to call their own. They didn't want an outdoor space that just looked nice. They wanted to spend meaningful time together. Aaron's plans became more than just another gorgeously done design and more than just another good story about how they could invite friends and family to join them in enjoying that gorgeous yard.

    Aaron had pulled all of the pieces together—and then pulled off a Hail Mary pass of his own when he added that one extra-special touch just before he headed over to the appointment. And like excited sports fans who retell for years to come the story of how they were there when their team scored the winning touchdown in overtime or made the half-court shot just before the buzzer...seeing their kindergartner's enthusiasm as he, too, got to participate in the design process became a treasured memory for Jacob and Natalie.

Key Takeaways

Whether or not a client has an artistically inclined kindergartner with crayons at the ready, there are quite a few ways to incorporate memorable surprises into a project.

The Design

- Does your client especially love their dog and their vintage blue car? Add both to your design, personalizing the car's paint job and featuring the dog on the sunny deck.
- Highlight a special feature, like the incredible view of the sunset from the new pool.

The Presentation

- Offer your client's kids line drawings from your design, perfect for coloring while the parents explore your project.
- Build anticipation by choosing "scenes" to pause on before revealing the next new element.

The Technology

- Incorporate "Easter eggs": sound effects (like the crackling fire pit or gently splashing water features) and meaningful details (like their anniversary year, etched into a decorative stone) make your design more personal.
- Go beyond the laptop: design on the spot with an AR-enabled tablet or invite your client to explore their space with a VR headset.

SIX

CREATE AN EXPERIENCE

*I like the dreams of the future
better than the history of the past.*
—Thomas Jefferson[107]

WHEN JESSE EXPANDED HIS CLIENT'S small outdoor kitchen into a complete backyard transformation, he achieved the goal set by many negotiation strategists: he made the "pie" bigger. Ten times bigger, in fact.

In negotiation studies, the pie often appears as a favorite illustration—because as a visual, it is so instantly familiar. The idea that follows is likely a familiar one, too: to open a dialogue or reach an agreement or sign a contract, everyone comes to the table, gathers around the metaphorical pie, and tries to get as big a piece of that pie as possible.

A number of researchers have expanded the illustration to suggest that just snagging even the biggest slice of that pie isn't quite enough. Instead, the best outcomes result from achieving what Jesse did: making the pie itself bigger so that everyone gets a much better slice. Geometry reveals the truth of that theory, whether the pie in question is blueberry, pizza—or even an outdoor living design. Answering that seemingly simple geometry equation, however, is not always intuitive. One reason: much of the work of improving that "pie" takes place behind the scenes.

The question of just what it is that results in a better outcome is not typically one resolved on the spur of the moment. Negotiation strategists have devised numerous theories—contrasting "distributive" vs. "integrative" bargaining, for example, or the "every man for himself" vs. the "I win, you win" approach—to help make that process both manageable and predictable.

However, much like Atul Gawande's checklists—which demonstrably led to far better outcomes when they were not just created but used—the route to improving that negotiated pie is often seemingly obvious yet curiously neglected, even by those who already know how effective planning and following a strategy can be. After all, even Gawande—who wrote the book on how valuable following his recommended strategy could be—didn't always follow his own advice. Instead of simply maintaining the status quo, a better route is to choose a strategy and—like Claude Hopkins, who constantly tested his theories, or like Brunelleschi, who varied his approach in response to his client's reactions—analyze the success of the results. One such useful strategy: create a fantastic experience for the client.

When Jesse expanded his client's project—achieving a 900% increase in the process—he combined listening skills with negotiation strategies, decision-making theory with good old-fashioned design skills. In so doing, he created a fantastic experience for his client at every stage of the design-build process. His approach in many ways mirrors the advice given by the well-known and frequently cited management consultant Peter Drucker. In short: if marketing is done right, the company will know the customer so well that the product will sell itself.[108]

Achieving that can be remarkably challenging, however—so much so, that journals like the *Harvard Business Review* regularly publish articles on how to manage the divide between marketing and sales. The titles of these articles—for example, "Why Sales and Marketing Don't Get Along," and "Ending the War Between Sales and Marketing"—suggest just how significant the divide can be.[109]

Researchers analyzing how to improve customer satisfaction often emphasize the importance of one goal that marketers and salespeople do tend to agree on: focus on the benefits rather than simply listing the features. Sean achieved that goal when he revealed his design to his client: he recognized that what she wanted to see was the custom pool that he had created for her to enjoy with her family. She would not have enjoyed reviewing an itemized list of everything that he had added to her construction plan.

Advertising executive Rory Sutherland suggests one reason why it is so important to understand what it is that your client truly wants—and needs. Sutherland—the voice behind multiple online speeches with views in the millions—makes the case that, sometimes, it is not enough to simply offer customers benefits to enjoy. It is also important to identify and improve even the seemingly minor issues that customers might not even mention.[110] Perhaps they are like Jesse's client Ken, who had given up on asking anyone to tackle his big, empty yard. Or like Lea's client, who consulted her after facing down unusable plans that didn't account for what was concealed beneath their seemingly wide-open property—they know *something* is wrong, and they need help fixing it.

As both Jesse and Lea recognize, just handing over a perfect design—a design that seamlessly brings together everything the client wants—isn't likely to earn a client's instantaneous approval. Indeed, numerous researchers have found that, sometimes, being faced with an array of seemingly perfect options can lead to stress, decision fatigue, and even anxiety instead of the expected happiness.[111]

To help clients feel genuinely confident about their plans—as well as increase their future happiness with those same plans—designers like Jesse and Lea create experiences for clients that take into account what their clients need at every stage of the process. After all, just as even the most highly skilled and experienced doctors benefit from following their own checklists—no matter how seemingly obvious the steps listed[112]—even the most experienced and highly skilled designers might benefit, too, from analyzing new ways to transform a good experience into a great one.

When More Really is More: What Helps People Feel Truly Happy?

The study of exactly what it is that makes people genuinely

Happy is a topic that appears with some regularity in everything from scholarly journals to click-bait social media posts, Ivy League classrooms to popular podcasts. The question is such a popular one that, according to *The New York Times*, one Ivy League class on happiness enrolled a quarter of the entire undergraduate class.[113]

Whether it's how to trick your own brain into wanting to floss or it's how to achieve fulfillment in life, improving the human condition or just making the commute a little less irksome—the question of how to achieve greater happiness (or, at least, reduce unhappiness) is one that philosophers and academics examine as often as consultants and advertising executives. What repeated studies have found is that just *acquiring* stuff—no matter how amazing the "stuff"—does not keep people happy for long.

One long-running study of wellness and happiness explores why that is. Since 1938, a series of researchers have been interviewing hundreds of men. After analyzing these detailed interviews, Robert Waldinger, the fourth director of that long-running study, has shared one thing that really does help people feel happier: good relationships.[114]

That conclusion might seem obvious: yes, good relationships are, in fact, *good*. However, their conclusion serves to confirm what many other researchers have also suggested: that good relationships aren't just nice to have. Strong social connections are linked (significantly so) to better health and increased happiness—and studies reveal that these effects continue well into old age.[115]

Beneficial as they are, relationships alone do not stand as the one solitary key to happiness. Indeed, numerous studies, taken as a whole, suggest that the mere existence of social connections is not what matters the most—it's whether those relationships are truly meaningful. That's why it wasn't the mere number of connections that Paul's clients Jason and Jennifer had made on social media that genuinely mattered to them. It was being able to connect with their friends and share with them a meaningful experience. This conclusion is further borne out by research done into what leads to better health or improved happiness, if just acquiring more money and more "stuff" isn't quite enough. The answer is experiences.

The distinction between *doing* and *having*–according to Amit Kumar's aptly titled study, "Waiting for Merlot"—is a remarkably important one.[116] And that distinction is one often explored—in movies and memoirs as frequently as in psychological and economic studies—by those who find that achieving what they initially thought of as "success" has not resulted in as much genuine, lasting happiness as they had expected.

One such researcher is Mo Gawdat, a notably successful executive who found that achieving financial success was not enough to make him feel genuinely happy. He suggests that achieving happiness might be a matter of actively reframing the equation—to take the advice offered in the title of his book, *Solve for Happy*, that is—instead of following the same old familiar patterns.

Much like Gawdat, who identified the need to reevaluate how he viewed happiness, Amit Kumar and his fellow researchers recognized that the link between purchases and happiness was one that could stand examining. Among their findings: although purchases seem more permanent than experiences, experiences make people happier.[117] Anyone who has purchased a new car likely recognizes the truth of that finding: commuting in a luxury car with all the bells and whistles might initially feel significantly more comfortable—but the "newness" of those bells and whistles wears off quickly.

As Jesse understood when he presented his design plans to Ken (the client whose project had proved such a challenge for other designers), there's value to be found not just in creating an experience and not just in helping the client see what experiences they will enjoy in the future, but also in helping build the client's anticipation for those amazing experiences. A custom swimming pool or a newly renovated landscape or an extensive outdoor kitchen might seem, at first glance, to fall under the heading of a "thing" to be acquired—but, as Barry Justus' pool on the cliff reveals just as much as Brunelleschi's 600-year-old dome, the "thing" itself (be it a custom pool or a cityscape-altering dome) is not quite as important as why it is being built—and how it will be used.

Indeed, in unique ways, Barry and Brunelleschi, Jesse and Lea mirror Sutherland's advice to pay close attention not just to the benefits to be featured but also to the "negatives" to be eradicated. Whether building a breathtaking dome or adding a welcoming lounge area, managing a crew on a cliff or working around a septic system—all focused their client's attention less on the technical details and more on how their plans would give them the best experience. In creating genuinely spectacular experiences, they reassured their clients that the design presented would deliver the results both hoped for and promised.

Herbert Simon and the Maximizers: From Good Enough to Awesome

When Aaron's clients, Jacob and Natalie, chose his design after growing attached to the line drawings that their kindergartner had colored, he recognized that the route they followed in arriving at their decision was one he would not have predicted before he gave the strategy a try. Of course, if his project had been less beautiful, or if it had not genuinely fulfilled their needs—then those coloring book pages might not have had so much sway, no matter how carefully chosen the scenes he'd offered up for their five-year-old's artistic interpretation.

Jacob and Natalie weren't like the ringleted child in the fairy tale, choosing between obviously tiered options. Nor were they choosing between three carefully framed and edited options presented on a home renovation television show. The bells and whistles were not what motivated them. What they were really choosing, in selecting a design, was a version of the future that they could see themselves enjoying the most. Perhaps the choice they were really making was between creating a backyard retreat and buying an RV they could use to travel during the summer. Aaron didn't need to sell them on the tech specs of the pool he'd designed. He needed to create a story for them that placed them in their future outdoor living space and helped them see why creating a backyard retreat was going to be a truly worthwhile investment for their family.

Helping his clients see how much they would enjoy their new outdoor living space was key for Aaron because, quite often, the choice that is really up for decision is not an immediately obvious one. Sometimes, it's between multiple options that might all seem rather good.

Offering Options that Lead to Better Decisions

The field of study that has become known as "choice architecture" takes a step back from the decision-making process to look at what happens before anyone is called on to make a decision. How options are presented can have a surprising influence on the decision ultimately made.

The concept of "choice architecture"—as explored, for example, by Richard Thaler and Cass Sunstein in their book, *Nudge*–analyzes how to make it easier for people to make "good" decisions. As Thaler and Sunstein explain, even when presented with excellent options, it can still be remarkably hard to choose. One reason, they suggest, is that it is not an easy task to predict how a choice will actually work out.[118]

Much like the math teachers who realized that many hidden

CREATE AN EXPERIENCE

steps lurked behind seemingly simple equations—and therefore that the process of solving those equations could be taught in a new way if those steps were identified and explained—Thaler and Sunstein went beyond the now-familiar idea that people often rely on shortcuts (or heuristics) to make decisions. They also suggested that recognizing and identifying these shortcuts was one route to "nudging" people into making even better decisions.

Putting Shortcuts to Use

Inevitably, of course, many decisions that people face involve multiple additional pieces of information. These pieces of information can be helpful—or they can muddy the waters. That's because people often rely on automatic mental shortcuts to make sense of what they're seeing. While those heuristics can (and often do) help people make sense of the world, sometimes heuristics can lead to remarkably different interpretations of the exact same image or option.

For example, a person from New England, where lobster is plentiful, might not hesitate to order the lobster special when a waiter recommends it. A person from the Midwest, however, might be cautious when faced with that same lobster special—wondering, based on half-remembered tips regarding which days are best to order non-local fish, if that special really is a good deal (or if it is just a way for the restaurant to move product before it goes bad).

The answer either diner gives depends on context. If lobster is plentiful and fresh, then there's no significant risk in ordering it. If lobster has to be imported, however, then the diner might use other pieces of information to help make a better (and faster) decision—like just how scrupulously clean the restaurant appears or how busy it is on a Saturday night.

Decisions like the one facing the Midwest diner can hinge on far more contextual background information than is immediately apparent. A restaurant might highlight their dedication to serving only high-quality ingredients in their menu or make certain that the public areas are meticulously clean. A designer, in turn, might follow a similar path. In order to help a client understand what they are really seeing, a designer might offer context cues. These cues—like scaled, posed characters or the family dog—help anchor the client to the design just as a detailed menu might help the diner.

The Family Dog and a Margarita: Anchoring Designs

Without context, it can be remarkably hard to get a sense of scale when looking at something new. Because people rely on mental shortcuts to understand what they're seeing, many optical illusions actually work by playing on these assumptions as well as differences in perception.[119] Adding swimmers to the water or a reader to the deck does more than just personalize the design. The swimmer helps the viewer understand just how much room they are going to have to play volleyball in the pool. The reader on the deck shows them how much afternoon shade they'll enjoy under their new pergola.

When a client already has a specific goal in mind—like when Lea's client wanted to float in the pool, drink in hand—adding figures to the presentation makes it easy to offer that experience to them well before construction begins. Because Lea also positioned the sun to reveal how the sky would change as the sun set, her client was able to easily see himself already relaxing in the evening in his new pool, favorite drink in hand.

Is More Really Always More?

One way of looking at the prevalence of mental shortcuts is to consider the intriguing idea put forth by award-winning economist Herbert Simon: "Satisficing" versus "Maximizing."[120] In the 1950s, Simon introduced his idea that people—like the organisms and animals that he studied in his paper—might choose to "satisfice" rather than "maximize." That is, many might accept the option that "satisfices" because it both *satisfies* and *suffices*. In other words, a person might pick the first option that's good enough rather than hold out for the best possible option.

His study cast doubt on prevailing theories that purest rationality could truly predict decision making, suggesting instead that studying behavior—rather than relying on strictly "rational" theories—would reveal far more interesting information.[121]

Always adhering to the theory of "rational choice" is a laborious goal—because (as research into communication reveals) people frequently don't have enough time, inclination, or even information to analyze each and every option, route, and suggestion that they are confronted with throughout the day. The New Englander considering the lobster special might be perfectly happy to "satisfice" rather than to "maximize." If that particular restaurant turns out not to make the very best lobster roll they have ever eaten, they can try another restaurant, diner, or shack—or even pick up some lobster on the way home and try their hand at a recipe of their own.

For someone for whom lobster is an expensive and infrequent treat, "maximizing," instead, might be a better option. They might choose to read reviews, compare menus, and double-check when lobster is in season before making a reservation to ensure that the meal they're about to savor won't just be good enough—it will be worth the wait (and the expense).

Tod Brown understood this distinction when he began showing his designs in 3D. When he first started designing pools, he used CAD (computer-aided design) software—which, he says, "was not the easiest way to sell pools." It was "difficult," he admits, because "most people cannot visualize a 2D drawing in their backyard." In order to help his clients visualize the end result, Tod supplemented his 2D CAD drawings with photos, saying to his clients by way of explanation, "It'll kind of look like this."

He very quickly saw that using 3D instead would help him create a new experience. Rather than asking his clients to look at a photo and imagine how it might look in their own yard, he began to create approximately ten screenshots of his 3D designs to bring along. Then, at the next meeting to reveal his design, he would share these screenshots and quietly let them take the images in, watching as they began to visually compare his design to their current space.

Tod's strategy is a successful one: in one 30-minute meeting, for example, he closed a $400,000 project. The client was amazed, asking, "Are you telling me that my backyard could look like this?"

The photos and 2D drawings he initially used had been more than good enough for Tod to build an excellent career. However, by offering beautifully rendered and precisely detailed 3D screenshots along with his design, he made it effortlessly easy for his clients to see exactly why his designs were more than just "good enough"—they were the "maximized" option that would give them the outdoor living spaces they wanted most.

Framing: Seeing in New Ways

A few years ago, the development team in our office assembled around one of the desktop computers that we'd been building. We had just installed a new graphics card—the most

CREATE AN EXPERIENCE

powerful one available at the time—and we were about to find out whether or not it would be powerful enough to view a 3D design presentation as a 3D movie, complete with theater-style 3D viewing glasses.

The results were pretty impressive, but as fun as it was to watch that 3D movie presentation, we recognized that asking homeowners to don movie theater-style 3D glasses to watch a presentation was not going to offer the absolute best or most enjoyable experience. Since the goal was to create the best experience for everyone, the option to use 3D glasses became something of another "Easter egg"—an entertaining bonus developed along the route to the fundamental goal: creating the most immersive and interactive 3D experiences possible.

Reframing a 3D presentation as a 3D movie had been more than just a fun goal to achieve. It had reconfirmed for our team that the most immersive experiences were the ones that did not just offer the results that were the most technologically impressive. They were the ones that offered an amazing experience alongside the amazing visuals.

How to create an even more impressively immersive effect without the disposable 3D glasses was not just an academic question for our development team to ponder—it was our goal, one that would soon lead to the development of entirely new tools, including virtual reality (VR) presentations and the first outdoor living augmented reality (AR) application, named YARD. Those new tools were especially important because we did not want to limit the ability to create the most immersive experiences only to those willing to tinker with their computer's hardware—or bring their desktop tower along to a meeting for a more powerful presentation.

How a presentation is presented and framed, after all, can have a tremendous impact on how it is experienced. In movies and novels, framing structures are typically quite easy to see and follow. Many familiar stories are framed within another story:

the search for "Rosebud" in *Citizen Kane* or the grandpa reading to his sick grandson in *The Princess Bride*.

Sometimes, however, adding layers and complications to a story just makes the story more challenging to follow and remember. The story of Mary Shelley's *Frankenstein* is a familiar one—and yet many casual readers (and movie watchers) sometimes forget whether Frankenstein is the name of the scientist or the monster. That the novel is framed by letters written by the captain of the Arctic expedition that discovers a wandering Victor Frankenstein and learns the story that will form the rest of the novel is a detail very few remember offhand.

When there is a lot of information to keep track of in a story, how it is presented and framed becomes even more significant. Just as people sometimes lose track of who Frankenstein really is, clients can sometimes lose track of the details in an especially innovative design that—however compelling the design or the story—offers them a little too much to take in at once.

The importance of thoughtfully framing a presentation or an idea or a story is not limited to the formal structure of movies or novels—quite often, in fact, reframing any story can have a profound impact on experiences both large and small.

In the summer of 2014, one charity proved the truth of this when it decided to rethink the usual method of asking for donations. Their strategy: instead of just requesting donations, the ALS Association asked people to donate…and dump a bucket of ice on their heads. Initially, some naysayers questioned whether the idea was nothing more than a feel-good spectacle. The "ALS Ice Bucket Challenge," however, quickly proved a success: in just eight weeks, the charity raised more than one hundred million dollars.[122] That feat is even more remarkable given that the charity had listed cash assets of just ten million dollars the year before. In just one year, their total assets increased 432%.[123]

As the idea behind the fundraiser reached a wide audience, the specifics sometimes got a bit jumbled—dump a bucket of ice or donate? Dump the ice *and* donate? Dump the ice on a friend? However, the suggestion to tag friends helped the challenge spread rapidly across social media. The money raised during that short period of time had a significant impact, helping to fund numerous research projects as well as the discovery of new genes linked to the progressive neurodegenerative disease.[124]

Reframing a familiar story for a homeowner might not reach numbers quite as enormous, but the results, as designer John Ogburn demonstrates, can be just as impressive. It is by taking the time to thoughtfully frame each presentation that John expands on the typical design-build process to help his clients feel confident that the luxury project he is designing is exactly right for them.

Clients, John has observed, want luxurious outdoor living spaces—and those luxurious spaces have become increasingly elaborate. The size and scale of such innovative projects mean homeowners sometimes need a little extra help following along during what John calls the "dream-to-reality process," so John has set out to improve that process.

John does this by focusing on building an authentic connection with his clients. It is not enough to just learn about the lifestyle or budget. Neither is it enough to just create a beautiful design. To offer his clients the best experience while also preventing complications from cropping up, John goes a step further: he also pays attention to any potential gaps in their knowledge base. Because John sees it as his responsibility to help protect his clients from making any potentially poor decisions, John takes care to balance his clients' wants and needs with their budget and their home's architecture. Then, when he shares his design ideas, he is able to help them not just see how his plan exceeds their expectations but also fully understand exactly how his innovative design addresses their yard's challenges—without requiring them to understand all of the technical details.

Thoughtfully framing his presentations is how John creates

designs that stand as beautiful works of art as well. To offer homeowners those beautiful, luxurious, and easy-to-understand results, John suggests that designers need to continuously adapt their approach. Indeed, it is by taking advantage of new products, new technology, and new opportunities that designers are able to offer a truly exceptional design hand in hand with an exceptional experience.

Whether sharing a good book, raising money for charity, or changing the scale of a project, reframing expectations can provide a better experience and also improve outcomes. Mary Shelley could have opted to tell her story a different way. The charity could have just continued to raise money on the innate worthiness of its cause. John might have offered his clients a traditional design.

Instead, Shelley sparked conversation about what it really means to identify a monster. The charity increased engagement by inviting people to share a fun experience. And John helps his clients rethink and reimagine what is really possible in order to offer them truly exceptional results.

The Sorites Paradox: Can Great Turn into Awesome?

A famous question in philosophy is known as the sorites paradox. If a pile of sand is known as a heap, and if that pile remains a heap after just one grain of sand is removed, then—if grains of sand continue to be removed—at what point is the heap no longer a heap?

No matter how one ultimately chooses to answer the paradox, the question itself highlights just how challenging it can be to discuss vague or unclear terms. Attempting to reach an answer might seem as comically frustrating as Abbott and Costello's famous "Who's on First?" comedy sketch.

For designers and builders, construction plans and 2D drawings are easy to read—when they're in context. At trade shows, after all, when our team shares that circular drawing with a little bump off to the side, even designers who were once art majors usually need a little bit more context—or even an extra sketch—to see that the circle-plus-a-bump drawing is not, say, a donut with a handle but actually a top-down view of a coffee mug. As soon as we show the 3D view, the cup becomes instantly obvious.

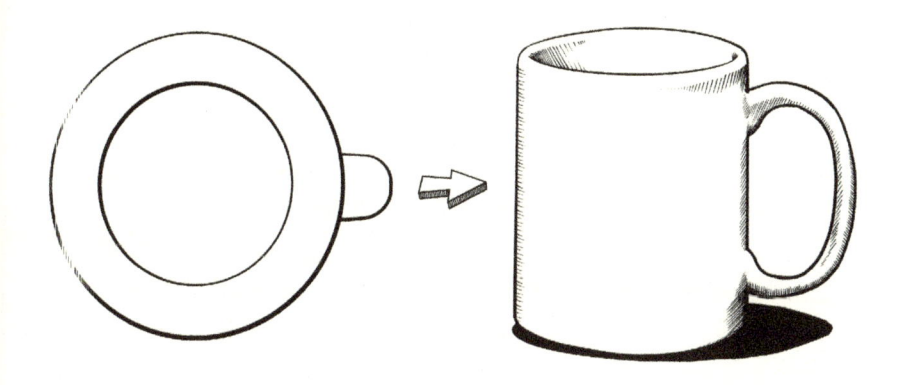

For clients, technical drawings and construction plans are often too challenging to fully understand, even with the aid of the most detailed verbal explanation. The point at which sketches become clear and designs transform from a collection of lines and arcs into a fully landscaped pool design is, like the sorites paradox, challenging to answer.

Much like the optical illusions that shift from a young person's face to an elderly one or from two mirrored faces to a vase, construction plans often become obvious only after the trick or key to reading them is revealed. However, unlike optical illusions, which typically present just one image to examine, construction plans and designs can involve so much additional contextual information that, even when the key is made available, the plans still remain opaque to the non-expert viewer.

Instead of attempting to analyze each and every detail, many, like Simon's "satisficers," might simply latch onto a good-enough interpretation. And, like the people advertising executive Sutherland discusses—the ones who do not always mention the "negatives" that are hindering their enjoyment[125]—many homeowners might not feel entirely comfortable revealing just how much they don't understand.

That's why, when Tod Brown shares carefully chosen screenshots for his clients to compare to their current yards, he takes care not to risk rushing to the next phase of his presentation. Instead, he gives them time to simply take in what they're seeing at their own pace. After all, as numerous researchers have repeatedly demonstrated, too many choices—even too many *excellent* choices—can lead to stress, indecision, and even anxiety instead of enjoyment.

Whether a philosopher is facing the question of when a heap is no longer a heap, a viewer is trying to discern just what some lines and arcs really mean, or a homeowner is attempting to answer what would take a design from good to great—when there is a chance that the audience might be overwhelmed by too many options, then paying close attention to how the decision to be made is framed and presented can turn the experience from a potentially middling one to, instead, a great one.

Presentation Strategies

Every year, our team attends trade shows—as we have for the past eighteen years. Some shows are memorable because we meet a truly fascinating variety of people—everyone from Rudy of New Jersey, who purchased his first computer at the age of 72

CREATE AN EXPERIENCE

so he could design in Pool Studio, to Sean O'Neil, who told us about the time he made his client cry tears of joy.

Other shows stand out because we are ourselves blown away by the response to awesome new technology. Case in point: the Vip3D virtual reality tour—which we followed, not long after, with the augmented reality app YARD.

When introducing new ways of sharing designs, we often learn quite a bit about what designers and builders are currently doing—or were doing. For example, we have learned about the many and varied ways in which designers are now incorporating drones into their design process as well as the numerous new (and sometimes surprising) trends that appear in different regions. And, occasionally, we also learn about the less-than-ideal tactics that some designers sometimes admit to using.

Presentation Strategies: What Not to Do

When one designer, Jack, stopped to check out virtual reality at our trade show booth, he admitted that he generally didn't even think about how he was going to present his designs. Sometimes, he told us, he simply emailed a couple of screenshots of his design to a client, asked them to let him know what they thought, and waited for their reply.

Occasionally, he sent a video.

His work was truly remarkable, but he wasn't getting quite as enthusiastic a response from clients as he would have liked. Jack was not the first designer to admit that he hadn't always recognized the value in offering a more immersive experience. However, much like Jesse (who expanded that "I win, you win" pie with his client Ken), Jack very quickly grasped just how much more he could achieve by introducing new experiences into his presentation strategy. As soon as he saw a design in virtual reality, he understood just how big of an opportunity he'd been ignoring: as soon as he took off the headset, he said, "*That was awesome.*"

Presentation Strategies: How to Build Anticipation

When Jack found himself surprised by just how much he enjoyed the Vip3D virtual reality (VR) tour, he arrived at one research-backed realization purely by chance. He wasn't the first designer or even the fifth who'd arrived at our trade show booth that day to try out the VR headset. Faced with a crowd, he decided to wait to take his turn instead of returning later.

As he waited, he found that his excitement was building—and he later recognized that the sense of anticipation he'd felt as he waited made him relish the experience even more. He was surprised to find that, before he even put on the headset, watching others react to the experience of seeing a design in VR for the first time increased his own enthusiasm.

In order to help build a similar sense of enthusiasm and anticipation for their clients, many designers choose to meet at least twice: the first time to learn more about the family and take measurements of their property, and the second to reveal the design. Other designers take this process one step further: some build dedicated theater rooms in their offices, complete with features like large TVs, projectors, surround sound, and even plush recliners worthy of the best movie theaters. In fact, some have even created special VR "staging areas" within these theater rooms to demonstrate how to use the headset and to explain what to expect.

When presenting in the client's home, taking note during the first introductory meeting of not just the outdoor space but also the ideal place to reveal the design later—be it the living room or the yard or the kitchen—can help create a great experience, too:

Bring along a VR headset

Showing a future outdoor living space in VR can help

create an immersive experience. It gives clients the opportunity to wander through a design and experience how they'll enjoy relaxing by the firepit and swimming in their pool.

Borrow their living room TV
Even relatively small living room televisions are typically far larger than a laptop screen. Skip huddling around even a 17" laptop and instead plug the laptop into their TV with an HDMI cable or connect via a digital media player to expand the view and make the presentation even more immersive.

Present on the spot with Augmented Reality
Fifty years ago, the first (partially) AR headset was developed. It was heavy enough that it needed to be suspended from the ceiling. Now it takes just a lightweight AR-ready tablet to show design elements exactly where they'll be built, simply by walking around the yard with that tablet in hand.

Turning "Great" into "Awesome"

A few weeks after giving VR a try at the trade show, Jack got in touch with our team. He reminded us that he was the guy who had often just casually asked his clients to let him know what they thought of the handful of screenshots he'd sent them. Ever since he'd walked through a design in Virtual Reality, he told us, he'd been unable to stop thinking about it. More than that, he had been telling everyone he met about the experience, too. His enjoyment of his new conversation topic confirms what Yale researchers have found: sharing experiences can make them seem notably more enjoyable.[126]

Jumping in and enjoying a pool is more fun than simply *owning* one, of course. Creating an experience is about more than just making the design itself more compelling. By creating that enjoyable experience, a designer helps their client not only see just how perfectly suited the design is to their family, their lifestyle, and their future plans. A designer can also use the experience to help build anticipation—and increase their client's enjoyment of the outdoor living space they're about to build.

That's especially important when encouraging an indecisive or anxious client. When there seem to be too many choices or too many confusing options, the discussion might start to seem as inconclusive as answering that sorites paradox—or as circular as an Abbott and Costello routine. Carefully distilling and framing the numerous options helps create an enjoyable experience for the client—one that they can readily talk about and share with their friends. Paul's clients, after all, enjoyed his design even more after they shared it with their friends on social media. Jack enjoyed VR presentations even more after he shared his enthusiasm with everyone at the trade show.

This highlights an important step in the process that sometimes gets a little overshadowed: all of the bells and whistles pale in comparison to the story of how the homeowner will enjoy the new bells and whistles. To avoid the risk of a meeting turning into a mind-spinning comedy routine or a seemingly endless Philosophy 101 discussion, it can help to put the benefits and experiences into terms that are easy to understand.

Consider the deal offered by a local pizza shop: a family usually orders one large pizza to share, but they notice that a coupon is offering two medium pizzas for the same price. For the mathematically inclined, calculating the area of a circle is the work of seconds—at least, as long as a calculator is at hand.

A highly motivated pizza aficionado might whip out a calculator to assess a coupon. Once extra toppings, free soda, or some garlic breadsticks enter the deal, however, even those willing to calculate the area of one pizza versus another might be less inclined to do the math.[127]

Most people often rely on quick heuristics instead of doing the math. They'll visually assess just how big each pizza seems to be when deciding whether it's better to stick with the large or spring for two mediums instead. In a quick survey, our team was split—and, upon investigation, it turned out that our team was divided in part because our favorite pizzerias offered pizzas of mathematically significantly different sizes. At some, a large was 16 inches—at others, only 14 inches. Sometimes the extra-large was 16 inches; elsewhere, it was 18 inches.

Pizza, after all, isn't regulated in quite the same way as, say, ice cream. The regulations concerning how ice cream is made, what it can (and cannot) contain, and how much it needs to weigh ("not less than 4.5 pounds to the gallon," for the record) are detailed in a document that currently runs to 2400 words.[128] Italian cookbooks might detail the process of how to make pizza in nearly as much detail, but the local brick-oven pizzeria is where families tend to go to enjoy pizza—not analyze numbers or study recipes.

And many clients—like Tod's, who signed the check for a $400,000 deal after just comparing thoughtfully chosen screenshots to their current space—rely on those types of visual shortcuts to understand and interpret what they're seeing. Tod didn't overwhelm his client with too many details or too many technical choices. He didn't present them with the equivalent of a confusing pop-quiz coupon that would have required breaking out the calculator before they even had a chance to admire the new features.

Tod, instead, made his presentation so clear and compelling that his clients immediately connected with it. They weren't distractedly trying to weigh a confusing array of options as extensive as a list of pizza toppings or quickly trying to do the mental math to figure out the numbers. Instead, they enjoyed the design he'd offered them so much, they were ready to jump right in and enjoy the experience. That's because creating a more richly layered experience helps the client understand exactly why that design will offer them the most enjoyment in the future. And that is an excellent way to make those metaphorical "I win, you win" pies even better.

Key Takeaways

Creating a memorable experience is just as much about axing the negatives as it is about revealing the benefits. People often rely on heuristics when making decisions, so take advantage of those mental shortcuts to make your design both immediately recognizable and incredibly compelling:

- Anchor clients to your design by including memorable and easily recognizable details. Adding swimmers in the pool and the dog on the deck makes it easy for your clients to see themselves enjoying the space you've created.

- Help clients understand even the most innovative and luxurious projects, at any scale, by carefully framing your presentation to make it easy for them to both notice and keep track of the important details.

- Take advantage of research that shows people enjoy experiences even more when they get to talk about them, and bring your presentation from "good enough" to "awesome" by offering your client an experience that they'll be excited to talk about with their friends.

SEVEN

SHARE WITH PURPOSE

Make no little plans.
—Daniel Burnham

Long before Barry Justus would use 3D designs to help his client see how his project would successfully be built on a cliff, or before Lea Frederick would use 3D to help her clients see how they could safely build around what might be hidden beneath their visually expansive property, artists and visionaries who wanted to share what they saw of the world had to rely on some very different tools.

Many of the tools that artists would invent and use to capture the best imaginable views were in fact inspired by an impulse that Barry, Lea, and so many other designers might find familiar: the need to share a meaningful landscape or striking scene from nature. That very familiar desire has inspired the creation of not just beautiful and lasting art but also innovative new ways to share that art.

Sometimes, the views of nature that artists were inspired to create and share were on an especially grand scale. In 1792, for example, the painter Robert Barker patented his idea for an impressively immersive panorama, which he called *La nature à coup d'œil (Nature at a glance)*, and designed to situate guests within a view that was both stunningly realistic and incredibly immersive. That same year, he exhibited a remarkable example of his patented panorama in London. Much like Brunelleschi's painting of the baptistery in Florence, Barker's panorama presented not a highly idealized view but instead a slice of life, one that reflected the reality that the artist saw while painting.[129]

Unlike Brunelleschi's painting, however, which was small enough for just one person to hold and view at a time, Barker's panorama was meant to invite many people to explore at the same time. His goal, as his patent explains, was "to perfect an entire view of any country or situation, as it appears to an observer turning quite round." In order to create that desired effect, Barker detailed exactly how the painting was to be created and displayed. He described not only how to paint shadows in the scene but also how to suspend the resulting painting and how to construct the circular building in which the final panorama would be revealed. The goal, he notes, was "to make the observers…feel as if really on the very spot."[130]

More than two hundred years later, while Barker's panorama no longer stands, a similar attempt to capture and share immersive "slice of life" scenes can be found at the Museum of Science and Industry in Chicago where, for decades, visitors have been able to peer into an extensive model train exhibit that now stands at 3,500 square feet.[131] The museum exhibit invites guests to walk through (mostly) to-scale depictions of highly detailed scenes from across the country. Like Barker's panorama, it engages viewers in part by inviting them to study the exhibit closely to spot surprising hidden details, or "Easter eggs"—like the figure of a superhero said to be hidden on one of the buildings—that help tell the story of each scene.

Other attempts at capturing nature just as realistically were not quite as grand in scale as Barker's panorama but were equally successful at reaching a very large audience. For example, less than a century after Brunelleschi transformed art in the West by introducing perspective to a generation of artists, the German artist Albrecht Dürer earned recognition for his often remarkably realistic engravings, drawings, watercolors, and paintings. Known as one of the earliest landscape artists, he is also known for his renderings of animals. His 1502 watercolor of a hare, for example, remains noteworthy for its detail, accuracy, and precision. His somewhat less accurate woodcut of a rhinoceros in 1515, however, was the work that would reach an especially wide audience.

Dürer did not have access to a rhinoceros to use as a model. Instead, he based his drawing on a written description as well as another artist's sketch. Before the invention of the camera, it was not uncommon for artists to base drawings on descriptions written by those who had traveled abroad. Some of the resulting works, of course, were more creative than accurate.

An illuminated manuscript from the 1440s, for example, includes many familiar and readily recognizable plants and animals, like ducks. However, animals that were less familiar to artists at the time, like the elephant, are not quite as recognizable. The elephant pictured in this fifteenth-century illuminated manuscript might instead seem to resemble a heavy-bodied horse with a very long, thin trunk and small—even *tiny*—ears.[132]

Dürer's drawing comes close to a rhinoceros, but it too is quite imaginative. His woodcut was so widely admired and accepted, however, that it was regularly used as an illustration of the rhinoceros for some time.[133]

Scholars attribute the success of Dürer's woodcut at least in part to its timing: it was an image readily reproduced by the printing press at a time when images were even more appealing than printed texts.[134] Equally intriguing to Dürer's contemporaries might have been the story of the rhinoceros that he depicted. Sent from India as a gift to the king of Portugal, the real rhinoceros had been exhibited in Lisbon for a time before it unfortunately drowned in a shipwreck. Dürer's widely reproduced woodcut therefore served to introduce many people to an animal that they would not otherwise have been able to see.

And in order for Brunelleschi to transform the Florence skyline or for Lancelot Brown to transform his clients' sprawling estates or even for Dürer to introduce the rhinoceros to many who never dreamed of seeing one, new ways of both capturing and sharing innovative ideas had to be created.

The Necessity of Curiosity: Discovering New Ways of Seeing

Some inventions are known more for their serendipitous origins than for the work that followed the discovery. Movies have frequently employed a familiar shorthand to mark such moments: *Eureka!*

Ever since Archimedes set the precedent—allegedly exclaiming *Eureka!* after he noted the displacement of water when he was taking a bath—inventors, mathematicians, scientists, and creators alike have been inspired by what they notice about the world around them. For all the frequency with which the proverb, "Necessity is the mother of invention," gets quoted, many intriguing, world-changing inventions owe a bit more to curiosity than to the motivation of necessity alone.

There's the engineer whose stroll through the lab led to the development of the microwave, after a bar of chocolate melted in his pocket. There are the caffeine-craving scientists who became known for developing the first webcam after they networked a camera so they could check just how much coffee was left in the pot before heading to the break room.[135] And there is William Henry Fox Talbot, the Victorian scientist and inventor who, in the 1830s, was motivated to invent an early form of photography when he was dissatisfied with his own ability to sketch what he saw on a trip to Lake Como. Visiting Lake Como, it's not hard to understand why Talbot would be so inspired by the view that he would also be inspired to invent a new way of capturing—and sharing—what he saw before him.

As interested in botany as he was in math and the classics, Talbot—like many artists—was a bit of a Renaissance man. He did not feel quite accomplished enough to see himself as a true artist, however. To make up for that perceived deficiency, he invented a new way of printing photographs. Talbot, of course, was ultimately not the first to invent the photograph. What he invented was a method to print on paper—and not just to print one photo but also to print more than one copy relatively quickly. The name he gave his photos—Calotypes, which means "beautiful" and "impression" in Greek—reflected his desire to capture the natural beauty of what he saw but could not quite draw.

What Talbot wanted to achieve was also reflected in the title of the book he later published, *The Pencil of Nature*. After his own attempt at wielding a pencil proved insufficient, Talbot turned to science to capture the beauty of Lake Como:

> *One of the first days of the month of October 1833, I was amusing myself on the lovely shores of the Lake of Como, in Italy, taking sketches with Wollaston's Camera Lucida, or rather I should say, attempting to take them: but with the smallest possible amount of success. For when the eye was removed from the prism–in which all looked beautiful–I found that the faithless pencil had only left traces on the paper melancholy to behold.*
>
> *After various fruitless attempts, I laid aside the instrument and came to the conclusion, that its use required a previous knowledge of drawing, which unfortunately I did not possess.*[136]

Talbot felt limited by his artistic ability. Even with the aid of a camera lucida, his "faithless" pencil prevented him from capturing the true beauty of what he wanted to preserve and share. But it also motivated him to find another solution. Instead of relying on his own ability to trace a captured image with a pencil, Talbot would instead spend a number of years inventing a new way of preserving and sharing the views of nature that he so greatly admired.

Talbot's frustration might seem familiar to anyone who has struggled to capture the full beauty of an especially scenic view. He described the beauty of the views he was attempting to capture as "inimitable," and the views given through the glass lens of the camera lucida as "fairy pictures, creations of a moment, and destined as rapidly to fade away."[137]

When Talbot developed his method of taking photographs, he shared in *The Pencil of Nature* his method as well as his results—and he did not hesitate to admit to the many other variably successful methods he attempted along the way. Perhaps like Paul, the designer who initially saw the stream of photos shared on social media as nothing more than a modern version of the vacation slideshows endured by his parents' generation, Talbot recognized that photos alone told only part of the story. As beautiful as the images he printed were, they did not capture everything he wanted to share with his audience. Therefore, he included detailed captions alongside the photos he printed.

In describing a photo entitled "Plate III. Articles of China," for example, Talbot hints at his method's limitations—as well as its possibilities—when he compares the paper to the retina of the eye: "The articles represented on this plate are numerous: but, however numerous the objects—however complicated the arrangement—the Camera depicts them all at once. It may be said to make a picture of whatever it *sees*."[138]

Recognizing the challenge of improving the view of what the camera depicts and "sees," Talbot offers suggestions that would still be useful today, including tips on how to manage sunlight: "sunshine causes such strong shadows as sometimes to confuse the subject. To prevent this, it is a good plan to hold a white cloth on one side of the statue at a little distance to reflect back the sun's rays and cause a faint illumination of the parts which would otherwise be lost in shadow."[139]

Nearly two centuries later, what Talbot refers to as the "New Art" of photography has become almost commonplace. Researchers have found more than three-quarters of Americans own smartphones—meaning most of us, therefore, also have easy access to a camera.[140] The enormous number of photographs taken and shared inevitably means many of these photos are viewed a bit like those vacation slideshows of Paul's parents' generation—easy to share, but not always very memorable.

That desire to share and preserve memorable views of what one sees is something that designer Damon Lang often sees reflected in his own clients. Early in his career, Damon began to realize that his clients appreciated beautiful images—perhaps even as much as Talbot himself did.

"A painter's eye," Talbot wrote, "will often be arrested where ordinary people see nothing remarkable. A casual gleam of sunshine, or a shadow thrown across his path, a time-withered oak, or a moss-covered stone may awaken a train of thoughts and feelings, and picturesque imaginings."[141]

That ability to reveal something extraordinary through a carefully framed view is one reason that Damon—an award-winning designer who has appeared on television and published books on landscaping—shares 3D images and videos of his plans with his customers. Early in his career, Damon found that homeowners often couldn't make sense of what they were seeing, no matter how much time he put into his designs: "Two-dimensional plans just don't speak to the customer." What did speak to them: being able to explore their own space, especially when revealed in an often startlingly new way.

In order to eliminate the frustration his clients—like Talbot—felt at seeing images that just weren't quite right, Damon sought new ways to help his clients connect and see the beauty of what he was offering them. Of course, unlike Talbot, whose "faithless" pencil proved "fruitless," Damon did know how to draw quite remarkably beautiful designs—designs that more than captured the beauty of what he had created for his clients.

It wasn't that his clients didn't think his designs were beautiful. It was that his clients couldn't quite understand how his 2D drawings could become their real backyard. Even the most detailed images that he was creating sometimes still stumped them. To help his clients understand how a drawing would look in three dimensions, Damon turned to the latest technology to frame not just the projects that he designs but also the stories that he shapes at the same time.

For Damon, it's that very ability to combine the technology and the client's story that makes technology developed specifically for landscape design so valuable. "It's like I'm producing my own movie," he says. "I can make sure the video gives the proper perspective that I want the client to see."

As soon as Damon began to reveal his designs to his clients in 3D, he noticed that they responded as much to seeing their home and their family as to being able to "walk" through their future design. "When a customer can walk virtually through their new outdoor space, it's a game-changer," he explains. "My clients are blown away that I am able to create their yard in this virtual environment and present a design that shows them exactly what their project is going to look like before we even get started."

For Damon, who uses detailed measurements and photos as the basis for his designs, creating a story for his clients with landscape design software is more than just a way to share with them an easy-to-understand 3D view of his design. Framing and highlighting the best views helps Damon bring the client inside their project long before it gets built—inviting them to follow their curiosity and explore at their own pace so that they, like

Talbot, can enjoy an experience that goes "beyond a mere souvenir of the scene."[142]

Creating Immersive Views: From Letters to Price Lists

Of course, not all landscapes are quite as dramatic as Lake Como, just as not all landscape art is designed to be shared on quite as grand a scale as Barker's panoramas, and just as not all art is designed to be as spectacularly visible as Brunelleschi's dome. Sometimes, views of nature are created and shared on a far smaller and far more personal scale. For example, a number of years before Vincent Van Gogh began the first of his many oil paintings, he would sometimes include sketches in his letters. In one such letter to his brother, he included a drawing of a view from the school where he was then teaching. He so much wanted his brother to share in his experience that he took the time to create a detailed sketch as well as describe the view.[143]

Today, designers like Jeromey Naugle follow both Barker and Van Gogh, Talbot and Brunelleschi.

As Jeromey understands when he prepares designs for his clients, it is that careful attention to detail that makes the difference between the merely beautiful and the truly immersive. Like Van Gogh, who wanted to share not just the scene but also the story of why it was so moving to him, Jeromey takes care to make sure he truly understands what it is that inspires and moves his clients before he shares his design with them.

When Jeromey starts to plan a project for one of his clients, he prioritizes the personal details in order to make certain that he is giving his clients a design that they will continue to love for many years to come. Their attention to detail is such that Jeromey's team would be more than capable of keeping track of all of the detailed scenes and "Easter eggs" hidden among the Museum of Science and Industry's 3,500 square-foot model train display. After all, not only do they carefully keep track of the personal details that matter most to their clients. They also maintain an incredibly detailed price sheet that includes more than 1,000 items.

That 1,000-item list is especially useful to Jeromey because, when he designs for his clients, he is thinking just as much about what his clients will enjoy in the future as he is about the challenges in their current space that need solving. His goal, he says, is for his clients to be even happier with the project he designs for them ten years later than they are the day they sign the contract: "It needs to be timeless and it needs to always be able to reflect them," he explains, "no matter what stage of life they are at."

For his clients to be as happy to, as he puts it, "sit there and stare out the window at their pool" ten years later as they are the day they first see their completed project motivates Jeromey to create truly unique and personal designs for each and every client.

"We have never built the same concept twice for any client," he says. One reason he is able to create so many distinctly unique designs is because he constantly looks to art, architecture, and design for inspiration and education.

In fact, Jeromey believes so strongly in the value of pursuing an education that he regularly shares tips, ideas, and advice with other designers. He frequently advises new designers to study design and architecture to improve their work. "In the pool business," he says, "if you've never done it before, you are going to be doing your customers and yourself a disservice by just starting to draw circles and straight lines and selling it to a client.

"If you don't understand architecture and you don't understand the balance, then you don't understand design or flow. [Without] these different important factors of design, you're never going to know how to make a customer's backyard function properly. You're never going to be able to push the limits of what you're able to do."

Pursuing education and pushing the limits of what is possible is especially important to Jeromey because it is how he grew his own business: "As soon as I started [studying architecture]," he explains, "my designs went from $50,000-$60,000 pools to $250,000+ pools."

It is through the study of art and architecture that Jeromey is able to make sure that even his most innovative designs work in a client's space: "Nothing," he says, "is pulling your brain one way and another way. It all just flows and makes sense."

Jeromey aims to share designs with his clients that go beyond the simply beautiful. Like Brunelleschi and Barker, he takes pains to create truly immersive works of art that reflect reality. And, like Talbot and Van Gogh, he also makes certain that those works of art are genuinely meaningful and personal for his clients.

The Appearance of Design: Make No Little Plans

Exactly what it is that makes art or design meaningful is a frequently debated topic. For centuries, people have debated the meaning of the *Mona Lisa*'s smile. And visitors to modern art galleries sometimes question whether or not the art contained within deserves the often remarkably high price tags attached.

Amit Kumar's research into the differences between *having* and *doing* suggests that debating these very questions might be an enjoyable experience in itself: talking about an experience, after all, is enjoyable.[144]

If that's the case, then talking about a shared experience

might be even more enjoyable. For example, it's far more enjoyable to talk with friends about a bucket-list trip paragliding in Switzerland than it is to chat about, say, buying a replacement couch for the office break room. Not only is Lauterbrunnen a distinctly beautiful location, but—as Anne of Green Gables might agree—it offers rather more "scope for the imagination"[145] than even the most beautiful furniture showroom is likely to provide.

In a famous quote that can be found scattered with some regularity around the city of Chicago, architect Daniel Burnham—known for his work on the 1893 World's Columbian Exposition as well as for designing New York's uniquely triangular Flatiron Building, among numerous other still-famous places—highlighted the value of such engaging experiences when he said, "Make no little plans; they have no magic to stir men's blood."

Burnham's full speech was recently discovered in a 1910 newspaper:

> *Make no little plans; they have no magic to stir men's blood and probably themselves will not be realized. Make big plans; aim high in hope and work, remembering that a noble, logical diagram once recorded will never die, but long after we are gone will be a living thing, asserting itself with ever-growing insistency. Remember that our sons and grandsons are going to do things that would stagger us. Let your watchword be order and your beacon beauty.*
> *–Daniel Burnham*[146]

Burnham's speech urged his listeners to be bold, even adventuresome, to "aim high" and share works that would stand the test of time. For Burnham, there would be little point in hesitating to share bold ideas: any such "little plans" would probably never even get built. And equally important, such big, bold plans deserved to be not just imagined but also recorded because "once recorded," they become "a living thing."

As inspirational as Burnham's words are, it's worth noting

that Burnham did not see spectacular designs—like the Flatiron Building or the 1893 World's Columbian Exposition—as the only ones worthy of being built and recorded. While he and his business partner built numerous noteworthy buildings—including some of the earliest, tallest skyscrapers, which required entirely new ways of building to be devised—he also is known for having built quite a few department stores.

Burnham's ringing endorsement of the value of creating and sharing beautiful, lasting plans—urging that a "noble, logical diagram once recorded will never die, but long after we are gone will be a living thing"—is reinforced rather than undermined by his understanding of the value of doing the work necessary to build a successful business.

Others, however, sometimes have been known to take a rather less open approach. In fact, as impressive as Brunelleschi's dome remains, the details of exactly how he and his builders accomplished it has remained something of a mystery, because he did not leave many records behind.

He did, of course, create elaborate models, ready for his prospective clients to admire from every angle. And he did, too, convey his plans to his team of builders. But he was perhaps a little too suspicious: because he feared that his plans, if revealed in full, might be stolen from him, even today researchers aren't precisely sure how Brunelleschi built the dome.[147]

Although his biographer, Vasari, attributes the loss of his designs to "negligence," claiming that Brunelleschi "made diverse designs, which remained after his death in the Office of Works" before being lost, Vasari also reveals that Brunelleschi had something of a talent for revealing information about his designs only when it suited him.[148]

For example, he hid the true design for the important staircase that was key to building the dome: "since Filippo had stopped up the entrance [in the model] with a piece of wood let in below, no one save himself knew of this staircase." One reason for that follows: even though he'd won the commission, "he could not prevent all the other masters who were in Florence from setting themselves, at the sight of this model, to make other in various fashions," and "many of his friends told him that he should not show his model to any craftsmen, lest they should learn from it."[149]

Even though he "was for ever making, on the slightest occasion, designs and models of stages for the builders and of machines for lifting weights," when one of Brunelleschi's rivals wanted to see his models, he refused.[150]

Brunelleschi's friends were not alone in their fear that his work might be stolen. Michelangelo, too, worried that his "enemies" were after his ideas. According to Vasari, Michelangelo destroyed his own drawings and plans because he did not wish to "appear less than perfect":

> *He had imagination of such a kind, and so perfect, and the things conceived by him in idea were such, that often, through not being able to express with the hands conceptions so terrible and grand, he abandoned his works–nay, destroyed many of them; and I know that a little before he died he burned a great number of designs, sketches, and cartoons made with his own hand, to the end that no one might see the labours endured by him and his methods of trying his genius, and that he might not appear less than perfect.*[151]

Other biographers, however, have suggested that Michelangelo destroyed his drawings because he worried that they would be stolen.[152]

Brunelleschi and Michelangelo were aware that how others perceived them and their art mattered—and Brunelleschi, who strategically planned his approach to ensure that he would win competitions, certainly understood the value of using all the tools at his disposal, be those tools scale models or humble eggs.

As Aristotle explained, *"Even matters of chance seem most marvelous if there is an appearance of design as it were in them."*[153]

It is by being strategic and making what Burnham might have recognized as "big plans," or what Aristotle might have recognized as a worthy plot, that artists and designers are able to not just create beautiful art and plans but also to share such meaningful designs that they will be worthy of standing the test of time as a "living thing."

Creating a Meaningful Wow Factor

While designer Shane LeBlanc understands the wariness that some artists and designers feel when considering sharing their ideas and plans, he has found that consulting with his fellow designers is one of the most important ways that he both energizes and motivates himself to achieve even more in his career.

"A fresh mind," he says, "designs the freshest work."

When Shane first started in the industry, he initially worked on relatively small landscape projects. When the recession hit, he and his team "had to scramble to do everything just to survive." He began designing outdoor kitchens before a few clients asked him to design a swimming pool.

"I kept finding," Shane says, "that if I wanted to do outdoor living, then I needed to add the aquatics side."

Although that decision to design pools was born of necessity, it ultimately led to a significant shift in Shane's career. Not only did Shane discover that he enjoyed designing swimming pools but, after seeking out an educational program to join, he also learned that swimming pools offered him the rewarding challenge that he had been looking for in his career.

One of Shane's instructors also inspired him to begin sharing more of his work. Shane was so impressed by the gallery of beautiful pools his instructor had shared online, as well as the accolades his instructor had earned, that he set a new goal for himself: "I said to myself, 'That will be me one day.'"

Within five years, Shane achieved and then surpassed that goal: "I worked and I worked and I worked," Shane says. "It was a proud moment," he shares, when he realized that an online search for his name began to return even more images and results than he had originally found when searching for his well-recognized instructor.

While sharing his work had helped him earn his clients as well as build his online reputation, achieving his goal also led Shane to reflect on his future goals. Building his reputation online and earning recognition for his innovative designs had driven Shane to share his portfolio as well as his ideas online. Achieving those goals, however, sometimes led him to agree to work, as he puts it, "very cheap" on even his unique projects.

His unique, innovative designs and beautiful portfolio have earned him such a solid reputation nationwide that Shane often travels from his home base in Georgia to design both residential and commercial outdoor living projects from Dallas to Beverly Hills, from Louisiana to Chattanooga and Nashville, Tennessee, and from Ohio to Fort Lauderdale, Florida.

When he first began building his career, Shane hadn't fully anticipated just how rapidly his career would take off once he began sharing his ideas and his designs. His decision to do so, however, reflects his understanding that it is through taking on new challenges that he earns the opportunity to take on even more exciting projects. "You're only as good as your portfolio," he says, because "you're being recognized by your portfolio."

Shane, following in the tradition set centuries before by Brunelleschi and Donatello as they explored the Roman ruins to inspire and inform their own work, recognizes the importance of looking everywhere for inspiration: "I'm always looking and looking and looking," he admits.

One such look led Shane to discover that using landscape design software could help him achieve even better results than just drawing by hand. "I always drew by hand," Shane says. While his clients certainly enjoyed his hand-drawn designs, Shane was looking for something that would help him achieve more: he wanted "that 'wow' moment or that 'wow' factor."

At first, designing in 3D did not appeal to Shane, because it was hard to imagine changing how he designed projects. "Are you crazy?" he asked his business partner. "I'm drawing by hand. That's how we've done it for years!"

Shane realized, however, that he was missing out by not trying it for himself. Almost immediately, he realized the potential: "The sky was the limit from there on," he says. "It was everything I needed."

To create that "wow factor" for his clients, Shane recognized, he could do far more with the aid of landscape design software than he had been able to achieve when drawing by hand. Shane very quickly tried all three options—Pool Studio, VizTerra, and Vip3D—and realized that the speed with which he could use Vip3D to design complete outdoor living projects also made it possible for him to reach his goal of designing for the corporate level.

"I can finish something in the course of a weekend, to give [corporate clients] what they need," Shane explains. That speed sets him apart from landscape architects using other computer-aided design programs, while it also gives him the opportunity to focus instead on the details that set his unique designs apart.

As Shane's experience reveals, sharing ideas is a proven strategy to build one's reputation. In turning to the latest technology to create ever more impressive designs, Shane both shapes compelling design stories for his clients and continues to build his well-earned reputation.

Much like Hopkins selling beer, Brunelleschi theatrically crushing the base of an egg, or Talbot dedicating years to perfecting his "New Art" of photography, it is the combination of expertise, dedication, and artistry that helps designers like Shane LeBlanc build such impressive careers.

Eyeless Birds and Norman Doors: Managing and Setting Expectations

Today, equipment as easy to acquire as an everyday smartphone can be used to capture remarkably good landscapes and photos of nature. Before such tools became commonplace, however, capturing views of nature required considerable time and dedication.

When Meriwether Lewis and William Clark, for example, set off in 1804 to explore and map the western United States, they relied on sketches as well as journals to capture what they saw—and, over the course of their two-year exhibition, they encountered numerous birds, reptiles, plants, and animals that they described in detail.

Artistic talent aside, no matter how detailed their descriptions, they could not include everything—and sometimes they left out details. The description of the "Heath Cock or cock of the Plains," for example, runs to more than 500 words and is accompanied by a fairly detailed sketch.[154] The information missing from that lengthy description has been turned into a classroom exercise by the Smithsonian, in fact: they invite students to listen to the passage from the journals before attempting to sketch the bird being described. As detailed as the description is, one important detail was neglected: they did not describe the bird's eyes.[155]

Of course, not everyone can be an Albrecht Dürer, whose 1502 watercolor of a hare is almost photorealistic. It was not until the nineteenth century that inventors like Talbot began to devise ways for even those with relatively little artistic talent to capture the beauty of nature that they saw while traveling. The tools initially at Talbot's disposal—like the camera lucida and the camera obscura—anticipated tools to come, including computer-aided design and augmented reality. Talbot was motivated to create a method that was even easier—one, indeed, that anyone could use. There would be no need to remember to include details like the bird's eyes—Talbot's camera would "see" all that was situated in front of it. Of course, interpreting what the photograph captured was still important—and, as Talbot himself recognized, framing and arranging what was to be captured still took some skill.

The goal of images like those that Talbot captured might be said to follow what earlier artists also tried to share with their viewers. Brunelleschi's wooden model of his spectacular dome, Michelangelo's small wax models of his beautiful sculptures, and Barry Justus's detailed 3D renderings: all place the viewer in front of the artist's careful design. In doing so, they create immersive experiences that make it easy for the viewer to understand exactly what they're seeing: a dome, a statue, a beautiful retreat.

These models stand out precisely because they are so clear and understandable—and they stand in striking contrast to designs and options that are sometimes far less easy to understand or interpret. Anyone who has had to pause and decide whether to push or pull a door will instantly recognize one such design conundrum: the Norman Door. Given their moniker by Don Norman, the author of *The Design of Everyday Things*, such doors frustrate anyone who encounters them because the usual visual cues just don't seem to match up with reality. Push or pull? With a Norman Door, the typical cues no longer serve their purpose and the door just doesn't work the way it seems like it should.

A highly observant person—or one who has installed many doors before—might notice the details that indicate how any given door is actually meant to open. If the hinges don't give it away, sometimes the wear pattern might offer up clues. However, when a visitor expects to simply walk through a door, being brought up short by a door that bangs against its frame instead of smoothly opening is a frustrating—and sometimes even embarrassing—experience.

Homeowners—much like pedestrians encountering a baffling Norman Door for the first time or like readers wondering what kind of eyes a bird might possess—might hesitate to make a decision if they lack sufficient context to feel confident about their choice. And when the decision is far more long-term than whether to push or pull a door, a lack of useful information can significantly stall or even halt projects.

That is one reason why designer John Kay incorporates the latest technology into his design and build process as much as his presentations. John recognizes that providing his clients regular updates and detailed images at every stage helps them not just feel emotionally connected to (and excited about) their future outdoor living space. It also helps them feel confident that they have made the right decision.

Sharing accurate information is so important to John that he uses drones to get the most precise and detailed images: "We also incorporate 4K aerial technology, which is awesome," John says.[156] "I've always been a big fan of pictures and videos, [and] it's awesome to be able to shoot the 4K pictures and videos of the building process as the drone is hovering over the crew in different angles. I can then share the building process with my client."

"They love it," John explains, because it offers "another perspective for the homeowner to look at as we are building." John offers his clients drone imagery alongside 2D pictures to help them "really see how [their project is] coming to life."

John shares images with more people than just his clients. On social media, he regularly posts screenshots, videos, and construction photos. Because he freely shares images, he frequently fields questions and direct messages from other designers, architects, and prospects. Two common questions from fellow designers and architects that he is happy to field: How does he design his projects, and what software does he use?

John is happy to encourage such conversations because he believes there is genuine value to be found in not just sharing but also discussing and exploring ideas. In fact, John's freely shared and detailed construction photos have sparked many conversations on social media with people who simply enjoy learning more about how various elements of his designs get built.

For John, concealing images of his work would be as useful to him as treating the method of opening a door as an insider-only secret. Plus, John notes, the compliments he receives certainly don't hurt: "It's neat to get recognized," he adds, especially "from people who are very well established." Well-earned compliments inspire John to share and discuss his work—and even help him refine and fine-tune his most innovative ideas.

"We are going after the jobs that are very challenging," John says. That includes projects built on challenging terrain, like a tiered infinity-edge pool built on a significant downslope.

It is that drive to create innovative designs for even the most challenging spaces that builds John's reputation with his clients. Because he is confident in his team's well-established ability to deliver the results he promises his clients, John doesn't hesitate to share his ideas on social media. After all, it's not an infinity-edge pool alone that sets his work apart. It's the complete design-build package that his company offers.

One reason John is able to offer his clients such consistently high-level service is that he spends a considerable amount of time getting to know his clients before he begins planning their project. "Some [homeowners]," he says, "know what they want, while others have no idea." In both cases, John interviews the homeowners and takes detailed notes before he starts to analyze their property. That process, which includes an elevation survey, typically takes two to three hours. Most of the time, John conducts that analysis alone, because it helps him take in the details without interruption.

Careful interview notes alongside a detailed property analysis help John offer his clients more than just beautiful designs. It's John's willingness to share and explore ideas that motivates so many of his high-end clients to trust his team to deliver.

And in so doing, John creates and shares beautiful works that achieve Barker's goal "to make the observers…feel as if really on the spot" as much as Talbot's dream of capturing beautiful views of nature, ready to be shared.

Share a Pizza, Share a Design

Sometimes, however, designers hesitate to freely share the details of their designs and ideas. Like Brunelleschi, designers might feel that the risk of having their ideas stolen is too great to share their designs openly. As Shane LeBlanc and John Kay demonstrate, however, sharing ideas widely is a great way to create a delightful, engaging experience for clients and, indeed, to also earn recognition in the industry.

One way to think about the value of sharing design ideas with everyone, and not just with your clients, is to return to the question of which pizza coupon that hungry family ought to pick.

Choosing a pizza need not be as complicated as answering the age-old sorites paradox. Calculating grains of sand, after all, isn't nearly as appealing as debating pizza toppings. If a hungry family notices that their favorite pizzeria is offering two coupon deals—one that offers two medium pizzas for the price of an extra-large, and one that offers an extra-large pizza for just one dollar more than a large—should they spring for those two mediums instead of the large they usually share? Or should they just pay a dollar more for the one extra-large?

The math reveals the answer:

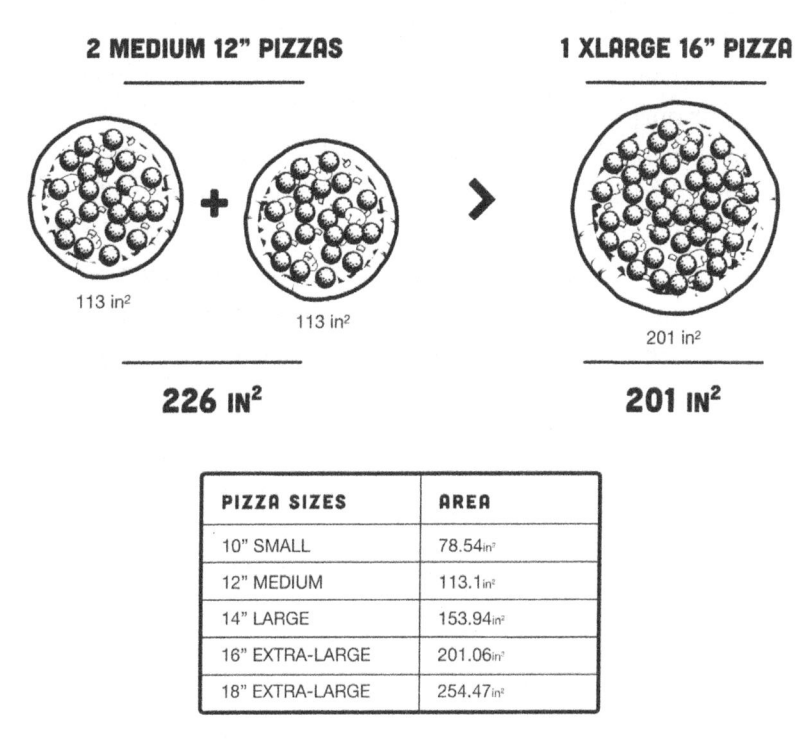

2 MEDIUM 12" PIZZAS   **1 XLARGE 16" PIZZA**

113 in² + 113 in² > 201 in²

226 IN²   **201 IN²**

PIZZA SIZES	AREA
10" SMALL	78.54 in²
12" MEDIUM	113.1 in²
14" LARGE	153.94 in²
16" EXTRA-LARGE	201.06 in²
18" EXTRA-LARGE	254.47 in²

The jump from a large to an extra-large might not seem that significant. And yet, math proves it to be so: a 14" large pizza has an area of ~154. A 16" extra-large, just 2" bigger, jumps all the way to 201—and that means that hungry family will get a quarter more pizza with each extra-large pie. Two medium pizzas might look pretty small next to that 16" extra-large—however, those two pizzas offer an area of 226 (113+113).

What decision the family makes depends on more than just

how hungry they are. Like Shane, who was so eager to build his career that he sometimes undervalued his own labor and priced even his unique projects "cheap," the pizza-hungry family might skip crunching the numbers and go, as it were, with their gut. Taking the time to strategize and measure the value of sharing one's ideas—or one's pizza!—can, it turns out, lead to better, tastier, and even more profitable results.

The end goal, of course, is not simply to optimize images or rack up likes or even squeeze a few extra square inches out of a pizza. What matters is your work, your portfolio, your career, and your purpose.

Like Talbot inventing the "new art" of photography because he wanted to share the beauty he saw at Lake Como, like Van Gogh sketching the view from the window to help his brother better understand just what the children at school felt as they watched their parents leave and like kids telling campfire stories to exhilarate their friends: telling stories, creating surprises, and designing in 3D is what helps you build anticipation and inspire your clients to keep the story going.

Key Takeaways

Nature has inspired generations of artists and designers to not just create beautiful art but also to create entirely new ways of capturing and sharing what they see—and what they want to see.

- Create phenomenal experiences for your clients by making the most of what nature and technology both have to offer.
- Keep up with the latest technological advances to amaze your clients. Brunelleschi didn't build his dome by chance; he earned the commission by drawing on what he learned studying Roman ruins and by living up to his ranking as a true "Renaissance man" of many talents. The proof of his approach still stands six hundred years later.
- Share the secret sauce that makes your work exceptional. If Michelangelo hadn't destroyed many of his sketches for fear his ideas would be stolen, the world might be richer. Take Daniel Burnham's advice instead: "Make no little plans."

APPENDIX

HOW TO CHARGE FOR YOUR DESIGNS

Art...
Will conquer nature.
—Michelangelo, *Sonnet XVIII*

One of the most frequently asked questions our team gets—*should I charge for my designs?*—is often quickly followed up by another one: *okay, so how much?*

The short answer: it depends!

The slightly longer answer: the pricing strategy that you follow is, of course, entirely up to you.

That second question—*how much?*—clearly reveals our positive answer to the first question that we so often receive. Our answer reflects our belief that designs are valuable. The story of the design that you create for your client is not a freebie tossed in to sweeten the pot. It's integral to the experience that you are creating.

The frequency with which we get asked that question inspired us to ask designers for their take on what makes a design especially valuable to clients. Insights shared by John Kay, Shane LeBlanc, and Jeromey Naugle reveal the importance of building an authentic relationship with clients in order to offer them an even more compelling and immersive experience.

However, in a 2018 survey, we learned that only one third of respondents regularly charge clients for designs.

The survey results also hint at an opportunity that designers who are not yet charging clients for their designs are missing: highlighting for their clients just how valuable their work truly is. Many designers today include far more than just a pool or just a deck. Hardscapes, water features, landscaping, outdoor kitchens, pergolas, and fireplaces are regularly featured in designs. A detailed, thoughtful design that gives homeowners the outdoor living space of their dreams offers them far more than just the shape of the pool or the size of the new deck. Your design is the foundation of the excellent experience that you are creating for your client to enjoy.

Zero, Two, and Five Ways to Charge for a Design

Very often, when new designers ask whether or not to charge for their design work, the person they're asking is JR Rapp, a Director of Business Development with more than thirty years of experience—and with more than a cursory interest in the outdoors. Whether hiking mountains, designing pools, or reading the latest advances in 3D technology, JR has long appreciated the value of discovering ways to make experiences enjoyable.

One of the many things that JR and I have agreed on from the very beginning is that the value of a good swimming pool is not merely in the easy access to water that the pool provides. Landscaping, similarly, is not deemed good merely because it provides oxygen. A great swimming pool or landscape design—or outdoor kitchen, or pergola—is far more than just the sum of its parts. Maybe the trees are in the perfect spot for reading your favorite Steinbeck novel. Maybe—as Jesse's client Ken so happily discovered—the outdoor kitchen offers a great view of the yard the family will enjoy while making dinner for guests. It is the experience itself that is valuable. And when the experience is so rewarding, the design of that experience is valuable as well. This is especially true when offering clients an enjoyable, interactive, immersive experience that goes far beyond a quick sketch of a design and that will be far more personalized than a typical "builder's special."

To help designers who are not yet regularly charging for designs determine which strategy might be right for them, JR often suggests a simple framework to use when deciding how to charge for a design:

Zero: Offer your design services free of charge.

Two: Charge a fee.

- Refundable: Offer to credit the fee toward the cost of the installation.
- Non-refundable: Treat the design and the construction separately; this means that you get paid for your design work whether or not the client decides to move forward with the project.

Five: Base your fee on one of five potential methods.

- Hourly rate
- Flat rate
- By acre/square foot
- By minimum project size
- By percentage of the budget

The method that you choose, of course, will depend on your goals as well as your client's project. In the follow-up to our survey, we learned that many designers who regularly charge for designs do so precisely because they recognize that what they are offering their clients is truly exceptional. They are neither trying to simply get their foot in the door nor trying to quickly complete as many projects as humanly possible. They are, instead, investing time to create something unique and personalized for each client. Perhaps they, like Jeromey Naugle, regularly pursue additional education to improve their design skills. Or perhaps they, like Jack, leverage the latest advances in technology to make their presentations ever more detailed—and ever more immersive. The experiences that they create are what make their designs so valuable to their clients.

Banana Shown for Scale

Computer-aided design has come a long way in just a few decades. What once took considerable time—and considerable resources—can now be accomplished nearly instantaneously. In fact, computers today are so much more powerful than when I needed to bring my desktop tower with me to share the first 3D pool with Buzz Ghiz that 70% of surveyed designers now use a laptop to create their 3D designs.

The portability of even the most powerful laptops today is suggested in another fact our survey has revealed: while 9 out of 10 designers prefer to design 3D projects in their offices, only 1 out of 3 also present designs to clients in their offices. Nearly half prefer, instead, to present their designs at the client's own home—and just as many also choose to make updates and changes to their designs on the spot with their clients.

Whether designing at a client's home or in your office, the very ease with which designs can be created not only in 3D but also now in VR and AR as well serves to emphasize rather than minimize the skill of the designer. For example, software now makes it easy to add true shadows to a 3D design. Enter the address, the time, and the date, and you can show a client exactly how much shade the new pergola will offer at three in the afternoon on a sunny weekend in July. You can even extend the presentation by heading inside their house and showing them, in detail, that the pergola won't block the light as they enjoy their morning cup of coffee in their breakfast nook. Knowing how to situate the pergola in the client's unfinished yard to create the best shade is an art—an art that can achieve stunning and extraordinary effects.

For thousands of years, the Temple of Hatshepsut in Egypt has stood as proof of this fact. At sunset, the light reveals the beauty of the design. During the day, the temple is certainly beautiful. Carefully situated as the temple is, however, it is at sunset, when the light hits it at the perfect angle, that it seems to glow from within. Then, the temple becomes extraordinary.[157]

Creating extraordinary and meaningful views is the work of an expert—someone who knows not only how to use the tools, but also how to use them to stunning effect. Tools, after all, are constantly changing: the first virtual reality headset was also partially an augmented reality headset.[158] Created by Ivan Sutherland, it was so heavy that it had to be suspended from the ceiling—and it earned a suitably weighty name: The Sword of Damocles.

Fifty years later, augmented reality can be used to present designs with the aid of nothing heavier than a tablet. When our team began developing what would become the first AR-enabled app for outdoor living design, we decided to give it a name that would reflect its simplicity, just as Sutherland's weightily named headset emphasized its momentous gravity. That first AR app earned the name that revealed exactly what it could design: YARD.

Designing yards—and pools and driveways and outdoor kitchens and complete outdoor living spaces—takes more than just technical know-how, just as telling the story of your design takes more than a readiness to chat with clients. And as Google and other researchers have shown, people will take steps to avoid unpleasant surprises. When a client comes to you, they do so because they're hoping you'll be the one to deliver on that promise: that you'll give them the incredible outdoor living space of their dreams.

Comparison shopping, however, is so easy—and even expected—that sometimes clients might not know what it is that makes you the expert they need. Websites and apps that facilitate automatic comparisons abound, making it seem easy enough to compare options. Whether double-checking a business's hours or tracking the price of an item to see if it'll go down, the curious can find information when it is widely and freely available. With so much information immediately within reach, however, it can be easy for someone to make the mistake of thinking that the lowest available price is the best available price, or that the option that looks the most promising will actually be the best one.

After all—whether it's pizza or pools, beer or cliff-top sports courts—people really do like to know what to expect. Sometimes, however, that delicious-looking pizza turns out to be far smaller than the pictures made it seem. Instead, be the banana shown for scale: the option so reliable and easy to understand that you are the standard against which your clients will measure all other options.

You, after all, are the expert.

Carefully selecting the pricing strategy right for your business and your clients is an excellent way to reveal the genuine value of an extraordinary and innovative design, earn your client's trust, and build stronger relationships.

Reveal the Genuine Value: John Kay

Designer John Kay makes the case that charging for designs is the best way to encourage clients and prospects to see the true value of his designs.

"I got out of the business of free designs a long time ago," John says. "When I first started in the industry, I was just trying to get work and I didn't care [that I was] drawing for free." That, however, proved not to be tenable long-term: "My time," he says, "became more valuable than that."

When John began to charge for designs, he found that the pricing method he used mattered far more than he originally suspected it would. Initially, John began by charging a flat fee for his designs. If the client signed a contract, he would discount the fee from the contract price. If they didn't, he still had been paid for his design. However, he says, "it didn't take too long to figure out that people would shop your number."

John believes that designs are valuable—and he also believes that designs are at their most valuable when part of a complete package. "When building a seven-figure job, I have to be out there quite a bit just to ensure quality control," John explains. "It doesn't make sense to not charge for the design. It is definitely time-based and difficulty-based."

"If someone came up to me for just a design, I'd probably turn them down," John reveals. That's because the high-end designs that he creates for his clients are complex, innovative, and challenging. By charging for his designs, John indicates just how valuable the careful, thoughtful design process is to the ultimate success of his projects.

Earn the Client's Trust: Shane LeBlanc

For designer Shane LeBlanc, who started out drawing pools by hand, transitioning to designing in 3D helped him earn his nickname: *The Outdoor Living Doctor.*

"The sky was the limit," he says. With the aid of Vip3D, Shane was able to achieve far more in far less time. Projects that might have taken a designer drawing by hand or even with another computer-aided design program weeks to complete were easy for Shane to finish—sometimes, in just a weekend.

Many of the projects that Shane completes are large enough in scale that the technical elements of the design often present significant challenges. Whether building an infinity-edge pool on a cliff, a Louisiana pool that is already at the water table, or one of his signature designs—a black perimeter overflow cube pool known as the Blackpool—Shane suggests that it is important to remember that a swimming pool is often the second largest purchase of a client's life.

"It's a pretty good feeling," he says, when a client trusts him with a quarter-million dollars to design a spectacular outdoor living space. Some of his projects are worth even more, with budgets for residential pools alone stretching to seven hundred thousand.

Earning his client's trust means that Shane serves as more than just a designer for his clients. As "The Outdoor Living Doctor," Shane brings together his training and his expertise to serve as the consultant his clients rely on to design and then plan how to build the project. Typically, Shane charges a percentage of the total for his projects. That straightforward strategy means Shane is able to focus on doing layouts while, he adds, getting out of the office.

Build Stronger Relationships: Jeromey Naugle

Jeromey Naugle, who started out in the industry stocking shelves at a pool store before turning to design, began to understand the value of charging for his designs early on in his career. What makes his pools stand out, Jeromey says, is his team's painstaking attention to detail as well as his team's focus on building strong, lasting relationships with clients.

That strategy works so successfully for Jeromey that his company does not need to advertise. Without advertising, he explains, "we did about forty pools last year with about a $100,000 average. And this year, we have already signed twenty-five pools and we are at about $200,000 average."

What Jeromey does not do, however, is share the full price upfront. In fact, he regularly incorporates into his designs far more detail and far more features than a client's initial budget estimate would fit. That's because Jeromey has learned that careful framing of his designs often motivates his clients to either build the complete design in phases or increase the budget to build everything at once.

"If I go all out on a design," he says, "and I send them a price at the exact same time, I'll probably never hear from them."

What he does instead is to set a flat fee for each design. For designs worth more than $100,000, for example, Jeromey charges a flat $2,500 fee. "That way," he explains, clients "are already invested in me. If they decide to do the project, I take the $2,500 off the cost of the project. If not, they can take my design and I still got paid for my work."

Jeromey charges for his designs because he understands that some prospective clients are very price sensitive. "That is just the way people are," he acknowledges. Jeromey further acknowledges that many designers are hesitant to scare off prospective clients. "In the long run," he suggests, "you have to start choosing your customers, [rather than] letting your clients choose you." Someone who will shop a design around to save $1,000 on a $100,000 pool, he says, "most likely wasn't going to go with [us] anyway if [we] weren't the cheapest."

By charging a flat fee for designs, Jeromey makes sure that his team still gets paid for their design work, and he also helps to establish with his clients that his designs are valuable. That policy works successfully for Jeromey because he maintains an open-book policy with his clients. It is one of the ways that he strengthens his relationships and builds trust with his clients.

Choose Your Strategy

When you are the storyteller of your client's design, you are offering far more to your clients than simply concrete and trees, rocks and water. With a nod to Shakespeare—the question is not *"To charge, or not to charge."* How you frame—and reframe—a story need not apply solely to how you put together a presentation for your client, after all. You might choose to take inspiration from the victorious Henry V, instead, and when *"the game's afoot,"* you...

"show us here
The mettle of your pasture."[159]

When you create an immersive experience for your clients, you do more than just offer them a great design. You prove the true mettle of your strength as a designer. Choosing a pricing strategy is just one part of the process. It is, however, an important step in demonstrating to your clients how genuinely valuable your designs are—and how much you have to offer.

It is your art and your skill that will help you conquer nature like Michelangelo and reveal your resolve like Henry V. Transform a property, blast granite, inspire tears of joy—and create an absolutely unforgettable experience for your clients.

Key Takeaways

Your clients come to you for more than your technical knowhow. An elaborate pool design, an inviting fireplace, and perfectly placed landscaping alone won't truly inspire your clients. What will? **Designing a story that will create an immersive outdoor living experience.**

Design for story

- Bring your client's outdoor living space to life by casting their family in the story of your design and sharing an immersive experience with them.

Earn your client's trust

- Charging for your design helps your client understand the true merit of your work. You help them see that your design is the foundation of the experience you're creating for them to enjoy.

Build great relationships

- When you design a great experience for your clients, you do more than give them a new outdoor living space. You help them build lasting memories.

NOTES

PREFACE

Benjamin Franklin, *Poor Richard, An Almanack For the Year of Christ 1738, Being the Second after Leap Year (Poor Richard's Almanac)*. Month: May, Column: 2. Philadelphia, Pennsylvania. Accessed on September 1, 2018. http://www.rarebookroom.org/Control/frapou/index.html?page=6

ONE: SELL THEIR STORIES, NOT YOUR DESIGN

Aristotle, *On the Art of Poetry*, trans. Ingram Bywater (Oxford: Clarendon Press, 1920), section 7.

Some names have been changed to protect client privacy. Any similarity to actual persons, living or dead, is purely coincidental.

Vasari, *Lives of the Most Eminent Painters, Sculptors, & Architects*, 9:80. Michelangelo's poems were often remarkably personal as well as evocative. "On the Painting of the Sistine Chapel," for example, begins, "I've grown a goitre by dwelling in this den" (Michael Angelo Buonarroti and Tommaso Campanella, *The Sonnets of Michael Angelo Buonarroti and Tommaso Campanella*, 58).

Vasari, *Lives of the Most Eminent Painters, Sculptors, & Architects*, 9:107–108.

Alcott, *Little Women*, chap. 27.

175

7   Robert McKee, *Story: Style, Structure, Substance, and the Principles of Screenwriting* (20th Anniversary Edition), New York: Harper, 2010, Kindle.

8   Claude C. Hopkins, *Scientific Advertising* (Chicago, IL, 1923), "Being Specific."

9   Hopkins, *Scientific Advertising*, "Information."

10 "Citrus: World Markets and Trade," United States Department of Agriculture, Foreign Agricultural Service, July 2018, Accessed September 1, 2018, https://apps.fas.usda.gov/psdonline/circulars/citrus.pdf

11 "Facts About Florida Oranges & Citrus," Visit Florida, Accessed September 1, 2018, https://www.visitflorida.com/en-us/eat-drink/facts-about-florida-citrus-oranges.html

12 Aristotle, *The Poetics of Aristotle*, VII.

13 Aristotle, *The Poetics of Aristotle*, VI.

14 In 2018, a dog was added to 19,887 3D designs.

15 Hopkins, *Scientific Advertising*, "Things Too Costly."

16 William Shakespeare, *The Winter's Tale*, act 3, scene 3.

TWO: MAKE CONNECTIONS

17 Andy Huang, "Introducing 360 Photos on Facebook," News release, June 8, 2016, https://newsroom.fb.com/news/2016/06/introducing-360-photos-on-facebook

18 Kristina Monllos, "80% of Instagram Users Voluntarily Connect With a Brand on the Platform," *Adweek*, September 28, 2017, https://www.adweek.com/brand-marketing/80-of-instagram-users-voluntarily-connect-with-a-brand-on-the-platform

19 Elisa Shearer and Jeffrey Gottfried, "News Use Across Social Media Platforms 2017," Pew Research Center's Journalism Project, September 07, 2017, Accessed September 1, 2018. http://www.journalism.org/2017/09/07/news-use-across-social-media-platforms-2017

NOTES

20 See, for example, Kee-Young Kwahk and Byoungsoo Kim, "Effects of Social Media on Consumers' Purchase Decisions: Evidence from Taobao," *Service Business* 11, no. 4 (December 2017): 803–829, Accessed September 1, 2018, https://doi.org/10.1007/s11628-016-0331-4.

21 Pew Research Center, "Social Media Fact Sheet," February 05, 2018, Accessed September 1, 2018. http://www.pewinternet.org/fact-sheet/social-media/

22 Mike Nowak and Guillermo Spiller, "Two Billion People Coming Together on Facebook," News release, June 27, 2017, https://newsroom.fb.com/news/2017/06/two-billion-people-coming-together-on-facebook

23 For details about Brown's work, see Eleanor Doughty, "How to spot a Capability Brown landscape at 100 yards," *The Telegraph*, February 26, 2016, https://www.telegraph.co.uk/gardening/gardens-to-visit/how-to-spot-a-capability-brown-landscape-at-100-yards/

24 Doughty, "How to spot a Capability Brown landscape at 100 Yards."

25 Celia Fiennes, *Through England on a Side Saddle in the Time of William and Mary, Being the Diary of Celia Fiennes*, with an introduction by Mrs. Griffiths (London: Field and Tuer, The Leadenhall Press, 1888), 5.

26 Fiennes, *Through England*, 23.

27 Evelyn Cecil, *A History of Gardening in England* (London: B. Quaritch, 1896), 270.

28 See "Bringing the view that inspired JMW Turner's 'Dewy Morning' back to life," National Trust, https://www.nationaltrust.org.uk/petworth-house-and-park/features/bringing-the-view-that-inspired-jmw-turners-dewy-morning-back-to-life

29 Evelyn Cecil, *A History of Gardening in England* (London: B. Quaritch, 1896), 275.

30 See Evelyn Cecil, *A History of Gardening in England* (London: B. Quaritch, 1896); Jane Brown, *The Omnipotent Magician: Lancelot 'Capability' Brown, 1716–1783* (Random House, Kindle); and Eleanor Doughty, "How to Spot a Capability Brown Landscape at 100 Yards," *The Telegraph*, January 28, 2016.

31   Evelyn Cecil, *A History of Gardening in England* (London: B. Quaritch, 1896), 270.

32   Horace Walpole to the Countess of Ossory, February 8, 1783, in *Letters Addressed to the Countess of Ossory: From the Year 1769 to 1797, Volume 2*, ed. Vernon Smith (London: Richard Bentley, 1848), 139.

33   Horace Walpole to George Montagu, July 22, 1751, in *The Letters of Horace Walpole, Earl of Orford*, Volume 2, 1749–1759, Project Gutenberg, https://www.gutenberg.org/ebooks/4610

34   Brown might have developed his interactive approach to presenting his ideas in part because he began his career as a "kitchen-gardener": "Brown, it is said, was himself unable to draw a line, and had had no artistic training" (Cecil, *A History of Gardening in England)*, 270, 273.

35   William Cowper, *The Task and Other Poems* (London: Cassell & Company, 1899), 137–138.

36   "Consumer Behavior," Google, https://www.thinkwithgoogle.com/intl/en-gb/tools/consumer-barometer-2017

37   See, for example, Merve Emre, "Uncovering The Secret History Of Myers-Briggs," *Digg*, October 7, 2015, http://digg.com/2015/myers-briggs-secret-history

38   Dan McAdams, *The Person: An Introduction to the Science of Personality Psychology*, 5th Ed (Hoboken, NJ: John Wiley, 2009), xix–xx.

39   If you are interested in trying the questions out yourself—perhaps with a friend rather than a client—the full list can be found online: http://journals.sagepub.com/doi/pdf/10.1177/0146167297234003

40   On the challenges of collecting and analyzing social media data, for example, see Susan Fournier, John Quelch, and Bob Rietveld, "To Get More Out of Social Media, Think Like an Anthropologist," *Harvard Business Review*, August 17, 2016.

41   "Overview of U.S. Renovation in 2016 and 2017," Houzz, 2017, Accessed October 01, 2018. http://st.hzcdn.com/static/econ/HouzzAndHome2017.pdf

42   Tracy Samantha Schmidt, "Inside the Backlash against Facebook," *Time*

NOTES

Magazine, September 6, 2006, http://www.time.com/time/nation/article/0,8599,1532225,00.html

43 "Internet Users in the World by Regions - March 2019." Internet World Stats. Accessed March 27, 2019. https://www.internetworldstats.com/stats.htm

THREE: YOU ARE THE EXPERT

44 "Art does not reflect the visible, but makes visible." ["Kunst gibt nicht das Sichtbare wieder, sondern macht sichtbar."] Paul Klee, Tribüne der Kunst und Zeit, Eine Schriftensammlung, Herausgegeben von [Published by] Kasimir Edschmid, XIII, Schöpferische Konfession. Berlin. Erich Reiß Verlag. 1920.

45 It is perhaps unsurprising that Kane's winning puck went missing again after the game and still has yet to be found. See Annie Sweeney, "Stanley Cup-winning puck has been missing since Kane scored," *Chicago Tribune*, January 28, 2011, https://www.chicagotribune.com/news/ct-xpm-2011-01-28-ct-met-missing-stanley-cup-puck-20110128-story.html

46 Bobby Hull once clocked in a slap shot at reportedly 118mph; see John Kreiser, "Slap Shot the Weapon of Hockey's Hardest Shooters," NHL.com, August 26, 2012, https://www.nhl.com/news/slap-shot-the-weapon-of-hockeys-hardest-shooters/c-640429

47 Jessica K. Witt and Dennis R. Proffitt, "See the Ball, Hit the Ball: Apparent Ball Size Is Correlated With Batting Average," *Psychological Science* 16, issue 12 (December 2005): 937–938, https://doi.org/10.1111%2Fj.1467-9280.2005.01640.x

48 Michelangelo is often credited with having said one of many variations on a quote suggesting that all he had to do was chip away to reveal what was already within the marble. This sonnet, perhaps, stands as inspiration for that idea—an idea that has also been credited to others, including the Victorian artist and art critic John Ruskin. See Michael Angelo Buonarroti and Tommaso Campanella, *The Sonnets of Michael Angelo Buonarroti and Tommaso Campanella*, Translated by John Addington Symonds, 1878, https://www.gutenberg.org/cache/epub/10314/pg10314-images.html

49 For additional detail, see Justus et al., *Pool & Spa Marketing*, 23.

50 For even more detail, see Barry Justus, "Working on the Road," *Watershapes*, https://watershapes.com/professional-watershaping/working-on-the-raod.html

51 Justus, *Watershapes*.

52 Justus, *Watershapes*.

53 For additional detail, see Barry Justus, Baldo Gucciardi, and Michael Flint, "Living on the Edge." *Pool & Spa Marketing* (October 2015): 19, as well as Barry Justus, "Cliff-Top Performance," *Watershapes*, https://watershapes.com/professional-watershaping/cliff-top-performance.html

54 Aude Oliva, "The Art of Hybrid Images: Two for the View of One." *Art & Perception* 1, no. 1-2 (2013): 65-74, doi:10.1163/22134913–00002004.

55 See "Table DL-20 - Highway Statistics 2015 - Policy and Governmental Affairs. Federal Highway Administration," U.S. Department of Transportation/Federal Highway Administration, Accessed September 1, 2018, https://www.fhwa.dot.gov/policyinformation/statistics/2015/dl20.cfm. See also US Department of Transportation, "3.2 Trillion Miles Driven On U.S. Roads In 2016," Accessed September 1, 2018, https://www.fhwa.dot.gov/pressroom/fhwa1704.cfm

56 D. M. Shaffer, A. B. Maynor, and W. L. Roy, "The Visual Perception of Lines on the Road," *Perception & Psychophysics* 70, no. 8 (2008): 1571–580, Accessed September 1, 2018, https://doi.org/10.3758/PP.70.8.1571

57 Shaffer, 1572.

58 Giorgio Vasari, *Lives of the Most Eminent Painters, Sculptors, & Architects*, Volume IX: Michelagnolo to the Flemings, Translated by Gaston Du C. De Vere. (1915), 107–108.

59 Robert B. Cialdini, *Influence: The Psychology of Persuasion* (New York, NY: Collins. 2006).

60 Thomas Aquinas. Trans. Fathers of the English Dominican Province. *Summa Theologica*, Part I (Prima Pars) From the Complete American Edition. (Project Gutenberg.) Accessed 1 September 01, 2018, https://www.gutenberg.org/ebooks/17611, 43.

61 Sheena S. Iyengar and Mark R. Lepper, "When choice is

demotivating: Can one desire too much of a good thing?" *Journal of Personality and Social Psychology* 79, 6: 995–1006. http://dx.doi.org/10.1037/0022-3514.79.6.995

62   Iyengar, 996.

63   Iyengar, 997.

64   Iyengar, 1002.

65   Michael I. Norton, Daniel Mochon, and Dan Ariely, "The IKEA Effect: When Labor Leads to Love," *Journal of Consumer Psychology* 22, Issue 3 (July 2012): 453–460, https://doi.org/10.1016/j.jcps.2011.08.002

66   David Bornstein, "A Better Way to Teach Math," *The New York Times*, April 18, 2011, Accessed September 1, 2018. https://opinionator.blogs.nytimes.com/2011/04/18/a-better-way-to-teach-math/

67   Robert Burns, "To A Mouse," 1785. The original reads:

The best laid schemes o' mice an' men,
Gang aft a-gley,
An' lea'e us nought but grief and pain,
For promis'd joy

68   Like Iyengar's review of the variables in experiments that led to her Jam Study, this story, too, perhaps deserves a little extra scrutiny. It might, for example, not have been the extra level of participation so much as the improved flavor of fresh eggs compared to dried ones that made the "add-an-egg" mixes a bit more appealing to buyers.

69   Norton, "The IKEA Effect."

70   Ed Catmull and Amy Wallace, *Creativity, Inc.: Overcoming the Unseen Forces That Stand in the Way of True Inspiration*, Random House Publishing Group, Kindle.

FOUR: DESIGN IN 3D—AND IN PHASES

71   Henry David Thoreau, *The Writings of Henry David Thoreau*, 373.

72   Brad Tuttle, "You Can Buy the Mona Lisa for $25,000," *Time*, October 2,

2014, Accessed September 1, 2018, http://time.com/money/3457030/mona-lisa-forgery-sale-mark-landis/

73   Robin Pogrebin and Scott Reyburn, "Leonardo Da Vinci Painting Sells for $450.3 Million, Shattering Auction Highs," *The New York Times*, November 15, 2017, Accessed September 1, 2018, https://www.nytimes.com/2017/11/15/arts/design/leonardo-da-vinci-salvator-mundi-christies-auction.html

74   Hat tip to the late Professor Charles E. Robinson.

75   See Beth Harris and Steven Zucker, "Linear Perspective: Brunelleschi's Experiment" (video), Khan Academy, Accessed September 1, 2018, https://www.khanacademy.org/humanities/renaissance-reformation/early-renaissance1/beginners-renaissance-florence/v/linear-perspective-brunelleschi-s-experiement and Ross King, *Brunelleschi's Dome: How a Renaissance Genius Reinvented Architecture*, Bloomsbury Publishing, Kindle, 2000. As Vasari notes, Brunelleschi's impact on art and architecture was significant: "Of very great advantage to architecture, in truth, was the new method of Filippo Brunelleschi, who imitated and restored to the light, after many ages, the noble works of the most learned and marvellous [sic] ancients" (*Lives of the Most Eminent Painters, Sculptors, and Architects*, 4:137). Vasari described the novelty of Brunelleschi's method in detail: "He gave much attention to perspective, which was then in a very evil plight by reason of many errors that were made therein; and in this he spent much time, until he found by himself a method whereby it might become true and perfect" (2:198).

76   See Vasari, *Lives of the Most Eminent Painters, Sculptors, and Architects*, 2:205–207.

77   Frank D. Prager and Gustina Scaglia, *Brunelleschi: Studies of His Technology and Inventions*. Mineola, NY: Dover, 1970; Vasari, *Lives*, 2:209–212.

78   For more information on the scale and expense of these models, see Hank Burchard, "Models of the Renaissance," *The Washington Post*, December 23, 1994, https://www.washingtonpost.com/archive/lifestyle/1994/12/23/models-of-the-renaissance/65f68385-53cc-49b4-85da-b9bd014b4b15/

79   As Vasari notes, one reason for the hesitation in choosing someone to build the dome was the fact that, sometimes, buildings were not exactly

NOTES

stable: "if some accident were to happen, as is wont to come to pass sometimes in buildings" (2:213), they did not want to take the blame.

80 Vasari, *Lives*, 2:197.

81 Vasari, *Lives,* 2:207–208.

82 Vasari, *Lives*, 2:208.

83 See Beth Harris and Steven Zucker, "Linear Perspective: Brunelleschi's Experiment" (video), Khan Academy, Accessed September 1, 2018, https://www.khanacademy.org/humanities/renaissance-reformation/early-renaissance1/beginners-renaissance-florence/v/linear-perspective-brunelleschi-s-experiement and Ross King, *Brunelleschi's Dome*, l. 520.

84 "[S]eeing the grandeur of the buildings and the perfection of the fabrics of the temples, Filippo would stand in a maze like a man out of his mind. And so, having made arrangements for measuring the cornices and taking the ground-plans of those buildings, he and Donato kept labouring [sic] continually, sparing neither time nor expense. There was no place, either in Rome or in the Campagna without, that they left unvisited, and nothing of the good that they did not measure, if only they could find it" (Vasari, *Lives*, 2:201–202).

85 Vasari, *Lives,* 2:198.

86 See, for example, Vasari, *Lives*, 2:261: "the Palazzo Pubblico della Signoria began to threaten to collapse, for some columns in the courtyard were giving way, either because there was too much weight pressing on them, or because their foundations were weak and awry, or even perchance because they were made of pieces badly joined and put together."

87 See Flavia Filimon, "Are All Spatial Reference Frames Egocentric? Reinterpreting Evidence for Allocentric, Object-Centered, or World-Centered Reference Frames," Frontiers in Human Neuroscience 9 (December 9, 2015): 648, https://doi.org/doi: 10.3389/fnhum.2015.00648. PMID: 26696861; PMCID: PMC4673307.

88 King, *Brunelleschi's Dome*, l. 726.

89 Vasari, *Lives*, 2:220.

90 Vasari, *Lives*, 2:220.

91 Kate Barasz, Leslie K. John, Elizabeth A. Keenan, Michael I. Norton, "Pseudo-set framing," *Journal of Experimental Psychology: General* 146, 10 (Oct 2017): 1460–1477.

92 Don Thompson, *The $12 Million Stuffed Shark: The Curious Economics of Contemporary Art* (St. Martin's Press, Kindle), 222.

93 "When Picasso Put Down His Brushes and Painted With Light Instead - Google Arts & Culture," *Google*, Accessed October 1, 2018, https://artsandculture.google.com/theme/lgLSm8J028B8KQ

94 See Pablo Picasso, *Guernica*, Oil on canvas, 349.3 x 776.6 cm. https://www.museoreinasofia.es/en/collection/artwork/guernica

95 Vasari, *Lives*, 4:100.

96 On his friendship with Donatello, see Vasari, *Lives*, 2:197–202. Vasari notes that Brunelleschi studied architecture because he wanted to be the one to build the dome, noting that he did not share his ideas even with his close friend: he sought "to find a method, if he could, of raising the Cupola of S. Maria del Fiore in Florence, the difficulties of which were such that after the death of Arnolfo Lapi there had been no one courageous enough to think of raising it without vast expenditure for a wooden framework." They were so dedicated to their studies that locals took them for "treasure seekers" (Vasari, *Lives*, 2:201–202).

97 For details on this story, see "The 'Gabbia per Grilli' Of The Dome," *Florence I Love*, April 16, 2017, http://www.florenceilove.com/the-gabbia-per-grilli-of-the-dome/

98 Vasari, *Lives*, 2:209.

FIVE: SURPRISE YOUR CLIENTS

99 Quoted in *The Bankers' Magazine of Australasia*, 10:562.

100 McKee, *Story*, 346–349.

101 Perloff, *Dynamics of Persuasion*, 295.

NOTES

102 Brian Lowry, "'Seinfeld's' Finale Ends Up in Sixth Place of All Time," *Los Angeles Times*, May 16, 1998. https://www.latimes.com/archives/la-xpm-1998-may-16-ca-50143-story.html

103 Jane Maas, *Mad Women*, 166.

104 The answers: *Hamlet*, in the end, remains a tragedy. If you have not yet watched *Rudy*, I won't spoil the ending.

105 Atul Gawande, *The Checklist Manifesto*, 187, 189.

106 Google, "Why people need to 'know before they go,'" https://www.thinkwithgoogle.com/feature/search-insights

SIX: CREATE AN EXPERIENCE

107 Letter from Thomas Jefferson to John Adams, Monticello, August 1, 1816, in *Papers of Thomas Jefferson: Retirement Series*, vol. 10, 1 May 1816 to 18 January 1817, ed. J. Jefferson Looney (Princeton and Oxford: Princeton University Press, 2013), 10:284–6.

108 Drucker, *The Essential Drucker*, 21.

109 See Andris A. Zoltners, PK Sinha, and Sally E. Lorimer, "Why Sales and Marketing Don't Get Along," *Harvard Business Review*. November 04, 2013, https://hbr.org/2013/11/why-sales-and-marketing-dont-get-along, and Philip Kotler, Neil Rackham, and Suj Krishnaswamy, "Ending the War Between Sales and Marketing," *Harvard Business Review*, July–August 2006, https://hbr.org/2006/07/ending-the-war-between-sales-and-marketing

110 Sutherland, *The Wiki Man*, ll. 824–825, 832.

111 See, among others, Barry Schwartz, *The Paradox of Choice–Why More Is Less*, 2004; Sheena Iyengar, "The Art of Choosing"; Jonathan Levav, Mark Heitmann, Andreas Herrmann, and Sheena S. Iyengar, "Order in Product Customization Decisions: Evidence from Field Experiments," *Journal of Political Economy* 118, no. 2 (2010), https://www.gsb.columbia.edu/mygsb/faculty/research/pubfiles/2619/Levav,%20Heitmann%20et%20al%20JPE.pdf; and Amitai Shenhava and Randy L. Bucknera, "Neural Correlates of Dueling Affective Reactions to Win–Win Choices," *PNAS* 111, 30 (July 29, 2014: 10978–10983, https://www.

princeton.edu/~ashenhav/Publications_Presentations_files/Shenhav_Buckner_PNAS_inPress.pdf

112 Atul Gawande, *The Checklist Manifesto*, 187, 189.

113 David Shimer, "Yale's Most Popular Class Ever: Happiness," *The New York Times*, January 26, 2018, https://www.nytimes.com/2018/01/26/nyregion/at-yale-class-on-happiness-draws-huge-crowd-laurie-santos.html

114 Anahad O'Connor, "The Secrets to a Happy Life, From a Harvard Study," *The New York Times*, March 23, 2016, https://well.blogs.nytimes.com/2016/03/23/the-secrets-to-a-happy-life-from-a-harvard-study

115 See, among others, Debra Umberson and Jennifer Karas Montez, "Social Relationships and Health: A Flashpoint for Health Policy," *Journal of Health and Social Behavior*, October 8, 2010, https://doi.org/10.1177/0022146510383501. James S. House, Cynthia Robbins, and Helen L. Metzner, "The Association of Social Relationships and Activities with Mortality: Prospective Evidence from the Tecumseh Community Health Study," *American Journal of Epidemiology* 116, Issue 1 (July 1982): 123–140, https://doi.org/10.1093/oxfordjournals.aje.a113387. Kirsten P. Smith and Nicholas A. Christakis, "Social Networks and Health," *Annual Review of Sociology* 34 (August 2008): 405–429, https://doi.org/10.1146/annurev.soc.34.040507.134601. Lisa F. Berkman and S. Leonard Syme, "Social Networks, Host Resistance, and Mortality: A Nine-Year Follow-Up Study of Alameda County Residents," *American Journal of Epidemiology* 109, Issue 2 (February 1979): 186–204, https://doi.org/10.1093/oxfordjournals.aje.a112674

116 Amit Kumar, Matthew A. Killingsworth, and Thomas Gilovich, "Waiting for Merlot: Anticipatory Consumption of Experiential and Material Purchases," *Psychological Science* 25, Issue 10, (2014), https://doi.org/10.1177/0956797614546556; emphasis in original.

117 See Mo Gawdat, *Solve for Happy: Engineer Your Path to Joy* (New York: North Star Way, 2017) and Kumar, "Waiting for Merlot," 6.

118 Richard H. Thaler and Cass R. Sunstein, *Nudge: Improving Decisions About Health, Wealth, and Happiness* (New York: Penguin, 2008), 172, 78.

119 Claus-Christian Carbon, "Understanding human perception by human-made illusions," *Frontiers in Human Neuroscience* 8, article 566 (2014), https://doi:10.3389/fnhum.2014.00566

20 Herbert Simon, "Rational Choice and the Structure of the Environment," *Psychological Review* 63, no. 2 (1956): 129–138. http://dx.doi.org/10.1037/h0042769

21 Herbert Simon, "Rational Choice and the Structure of the Environment." *Psychological Review* 63, no. 2 (1956): 129–138. http://dx.doi.org/10.1037/h0042769

22 "Every Drop Adds Up," The ALS Association, http://www.alsa.org/fight-als/ice-bucket-challenge.html

23 "The Amyotrophic Lateral Sclerosis Association Financial Statements, January 31, 2015, and 2014," The ALS Association, Long Beach, CA: May 10, 2015, http://www.alsa.org/assets/pdfs/fye15_fin_statement.pdf

24 The ALS Association, "ALS Ice Bucket Challenge Donations Lead to Significant Gene Discovery," News release, July 25, 2016, http://www.alsa.org/news/media/press-releases/significant-gene-discovery-072516.html

25 Sutherland, *The Wiki Man*, ll. 824–825, 832.

26 Erica J. Boothby, Margaret S. Clark, and John A. Bargh, "Shared Experiences Are Amplified," *Psychological Science* 25, Issue 12 (2014), doi.org/10.1177/0956797614551162

27 Not inclined to do a little math? The answer is shared in the next chapter.

28 "Ice Cream and Frozen Custard," Electronic Code of Federal Regulations, Title 21: Food and Drugs, Part 135: Frozen Desserts, Subpart B: Requirements for Specific Standardized Frozen Desserts (March 28, 2019), https://www.ecfr.gov/cgi-bin/text-idx?SID=15847527757c4a5a58ad43d489be04d8&mc=true&node=se21.2.135_1110&rgn=div8

SEVEN: SHARE WITH PURPOSE

29 Robert Barker, *Patent for Displaying Views of Nature* (1787), The Repertory of Arts and Manufactures, London, 1796.

30 See Barker, *Patent*, 167. Examples of an eighteenth-century panorama

are available online through the British Library: Henry Aston Barker, *A series of eight views forming a panorama of the celebrated city of Constantinople and its' environs, taken from the town of Galata, by Henry Aston Barker, and exhibited in his Great Rotunda, Leicester Square* (London: Thomas Palser, 1813), https://www.bl.uk/collection-items/panorama-of-constantinople

131 "Be Transported," Museum of Science and Industry, February 29, 2016. https://www.msichicago.org/explore/whats-here/exhibits/great-train-story/

132 Examples of illuminated manuscripts are available through the British Library: https://www.bl.uk/catalogues/illuminatedmanuscripts/. See, for example, plants https://www.bl.uk/catalogues/illuminatedmanuscripts/welcome.htm, a duck https://www.bl.uk/catalogues/illuminatedmanuscripts/ILLUMIN.ASP?Size=mid&IllID=49270, and that elephant https://www.bl.uk/catalogues/illuminatedmanuscripts/ILLUMIN.ASP?Size=mid&IllID=49254

133 Giovanni Garcia-Fenech, "Dürer and the elusive rhino," *The Artstor Blog*, February 11, 2014.

134 Jesse Feiman, "The Matrix and the Meaning in Dürer's Rhinoceros," *Art in Print* 2, no. 4 (2012): 22–26, http://www.jstor.org/stable/43047078

135 See both "Melted Chocolate to Microwave: An imaginative engineer turned a mess into a universal machine," *Technology Review*, January 1, 1999, https://www.technologyreview.com/s/400335/melted-chocolate-to-microwave/ and Rebecca Kesby, "How the world's first webcam made a coffee pot famous," BBC News, November 22, 2012, https://www.bbc.com/news/technology-20439301

136 William Henry Fox Talbot, *The Pencil of Nature* (London: Longman, Brown, Green and Longmans, 1844), "Brief Historical Sketch of the Invention of the Art."

137 Talbot, *The Pencil of Nature*, "Brief Historical Sketch of the Invention of the Art."

138 Talbot, *The Pencil of Nature*, Plate III. Articles of China; emphasis in original.

139 Talbot, *The Pencil of Nature*, Plate V. Bust of Patroclus.

NOTES

140 "Mobile Fact Sheet," Pew Research Center, February 5, 2018, https://www.pewinternet.org/fact-sheet/mobile/

141 Talbot, *The Pencil of Nature*, Plate VI. The Open Door.

142 Talbot, *The Pencil of Nature*, "Brief Historical Sketch of the Invention of the Art."

143 Vincent van Gogh to Theo van Gogh, Ramsgate, May 31, 1876.

144 Amit Kumar, Matthew A. Killingsworth, and Thomas Gilovich, "Waiting for Merlot: Anticipatory Consumption of Experiential and Material Purchases," *Psychological Science* 25, Issue 10 (2014), https://doi.org/10.1177/0956797614546556

145 Lucy Maud Montgomery, *Anne of Green Gables*, chap 2.

146 Daniel Burnham, "Stirred By Burnham, Democracy Champion," *Chicago Record-Herald*, Oct 15, 1910. The full text of Burnham's speech was located in 2019 by Adam Selzer, who published the details on his blog: "Burnham's "Make No Little Plans" Quote: Apocryphal No More!" Mysterious Chicago Tours, March 3, 2019, http://mysteriouschicago.com/finding-daniel-burnhams-no-little-plans-quote/. For the history of Burnham's speech, see "A Chicago tale: Why we're happy to erase the asterisk from Daniel Burnham's 'Make no little plans*'," *Chicago Tribune*, March 6, 2019, https://www.chicagotribune.com/opinion/editorials/ct-edit-daniel-burnham-quote-20190305-story.html

147 For insight into how one architect, Massimo Ricci, believes Brunelleschi built the dome, see Tom Mueller, "Mystery of Florence's Cathedral Dome May Be Solved," *National Geographic*, February 10, 2014, https://news.nationalgeographic.com/news/2014/02/140210-duomo-florence-brunelleschi-cathedral-architecture/

148 Giorgio Vasari, *Lives of the Most Eminent Painters Sculptors and Architects*, 2:221.

149 Vasari, *Lives*, 2:221–22.

150 Vasari, *Lives*, 2:218, 214.

151 Vasari, *Lives*, 9:104.

152 Carolyn Vaughn, *Michelangelo's Notebooks*, 7–8.

153 Aristotle, *On the Art of Poetry*, translated by Ingram Bywater (Oxford: Clarendon Press, 1920), 9.

154 William Clark, "March 2, 1806," *The Journals of Lewis and Clark*, 1804–1806. An image of the sketched bird is available from the Missouri Historical Society at https://lewisandclarkjournals.unl.edu/item/lc.jrn.1806-03-02

155 Evelyn Porreca Vuko, "Animal Encounters," Smithsonian Education, 2013, http://www.smithsonianeducation.org/educators/lesson_plans/lewis_clark/lesson1_main.html

156 Drones are capable of taking 4K and ultra-high-resolution images. A traditional high-definition display—such as a commonly available television—offers 1920 x 1080 pixels (often described as "1080p.") Ultra-high-definition resolution, which can mean 3840 x 2160 pixels or even 4096 x 2160 pixels, therefore offers four times as many pixels as a traditional high-definition image or display. In fact, it offers more than eight million total pixels instead of the two million offered by high-definition resolution.

APPENDIX: HOW TO CHARGE FOR YOUR DESIGNS

157 See Gulnaz Khan, "This Temple Honors the Egyptian Queen Who Ruled As King," *National Geographic*, https://www.nationalgeographic.com/travel/destinations/africa/egypt/luxor-temple-of-hatshepsut-theban-necropolis/

158 Ivan Sutherland, "The Ultimate Display," *Proceedings of IFIP* 65, vol 2 (1965): 506–508.

159 William Shakespeare, *Henry V*, act 3, scene 1.

BIBLIOGRAPHY

PREFACE

Franklin, Benjamin. *Poor Richard, An Almanack For the Year of Christ 1738, Being the Second after Leap Year (Poor Richard's Almanac)*. Month: May, Column: 2. Philadelphia, Pennsylvania. Accessed on September 1, 2018. http://www.rarebookroom.org/Control/frapou/index.html?page=6

ONE: SELL THEIR STORIES, NOT YOUR DESIGN

Alcott, Louisa May. *Little Women*. New York, NY: Library of America, 2005.

Aristotle, *On the Art of Poetry*. Translated by Ingram Bywater. Oxford: Clarendon Press, 1920.

Buonarroti, Michael Angelo and Tommaso Campanella. *The Sonnets of Michael Angelo Buonarroti and Tommaso Campanella*. Translated by John Addington Symonds. 1878.

"Citrus: World Markets and Trade." United States Department of Agriculture. Foreign Agricultural Service. July 2018. Accessed September 1, 2018.

https://apps.fas.usda.gov/psdonline/circulars/citrus.pdf

"Facts About Florida Oranges & Citrus." Visit Florida. Accessed September 1, 2018. https://www.visitflorida.com/en-us/eat-drink/facts-about-florida-citrus-oranges.html.

Hopkins, Claude C. *Scientific Advertising*. Chicago, IL, 1923.

Lennon, Thomas and Robert Ben Garant. *Writing Movies for Fun and Profit: How We Made a Billion Dollars at the Box Office and You Can, Too!* Touchstone. Kindle.

McKee, Robert. *Story: Style, Structure, Substance, and the Principles of Screenwriting*: (20th Anniversary Edition). New York: Harper, 2010, Kindle.

Sweeney, Annie. "Stanley Cup-winning puck has been missing since Kane scored." *Chicago Tribune*, January 28, 2011, https://www.chicagotribune.com/news/ct-xpm-2011-01-28-ct-met-missing-stanley-cup-puck-20110128-story.html.

Vasari, Giorgio. *Lives of the Most Eminent Painters Sculptors and Architects*. Volume IV: Filippino Lippi to Domenico Puligo. Translated by Gaston du C. De Vere. 1913.

Vasari, Giorgio. *Lives of the Most Eminent Painters, Sculptors, & Architects*. Volume IX: Michelagnolo to the Flemings. Translated by Gaston Du C. De Vere. 1915.

TWO: MAKE CONNECTIONS

Aron, Arthur, Edward Melinat, Elaine N. Aron, Robert Darrin Vallone, and Renee J. Bator. "The Experimental Generation of Interpersonal Closeness: A Procedure and Some Preliminary Findings." *Personality and Social Psychology Bulletin* 23, no. 4 (1997): 363–77. doi:10.1177/0146167297234003.

"Bringing the view that inspired JMW Turner's 'Dewy Morning' back to life." National Trust. https://www.nationaltrust.org.uk/petworth-house-and-park/features/bringing-the-view-that-inspired-jmw-turners-dewy-morning-back-to-life.

Brown, Jane. *The Omnipotent Magician: Lancelot 'Capability' Brown, 1716–1783*. London: Random House, 2011. Kindle.

Carnegie, Dale. *How to Win Friends and Influence People*. New York, NY: Pocket Books, (1936) 1998.

Cecil, Evelyn. *A History of Gardening in England*. London: B. Quaritch, 1896

Cowper, William. *The Task and Other Poems.* London: Cassell & Company, 1899.

Doughty, Eleanor. "How to Spot a Capability Brown Landscape at 100 Yards." *The Telegraph.* February 26, 2016. Accessed September 1, 2018. https://www.telegraph.co.uk/gardening/gardens-to-visit/how-to-spot-a-capability-brown-landscape-at-100-yards/.

Emre, Merve. "Uncovering The Secret History Of Myers-Briggs." *Digg.* October 7, 2015. http://digg.com/2015/myers-briggs-secret-history.

Fiennes, Celia. *Through England on a Side Saddle in the Time of William and Mary, Being the Diary of Celia Fiennes.* With an introduction by Mrs. Griffiths. London: Field and Tuer, The Leadenhall Press, 1888.

Fournier, Susan, John Quelch, and Bob Rietveld. "To Get More Out of Social Media, Think Like an Anthropologist." *Harvard Business Review.* August 17, 2016.

Huang, Andy. "Introducing 360 Photos on Facebook." News release, June 8, 2016, https://newsroom.fb.com/news/2016/06/introducing-360-photos-on-facebook.

"Internet Users in the World by Regions - March 2019." Internet World Stats. Accessed March 21, 2019. https://www.internetworldstats.com/stats.htm.

Kwahk, Kee-Young and Byoungsoo Kim. "Effects of Social Media on Consumers' Purchase Decisions: Evidence from Taobao." *Service Business* 11, no. 4 (December 2017): 803–829. Accessed September 1, 2018. https://doi.org/10.1007/s11628-016-0331-4.

McAdams, Dan. *The Person: An Introduction to the Science of Personality Psychology.* 5th Ed. Hoboken, NJ: John Wiley, 2009.

Monllos, Kristina. "80% of Instagram Users Voluntarily Connect With a Brand on the Platform." *Adweek.* September 28, 2017. Accessed September 1, 2018. http://www.adweek.com/brand-marketing/80-of-instagram-users-voluntarily-connect-with-a-brand-on-the-platform/.

Nowak, Mike, and Guillermo Spiller. "Two Billion People Coming Together on Facebook." News release, June 27, 2017, https://newsroom.fb.com/news/2017/06/two-billion-people-coming-together-on-facebook.

"Overview of U.S. Renovation in 2016 and 2017." Houzz. 2017. Accessed

October 01, 2018. http://st.hzcdn.com/static/econ/HouzzAndHome2017.pdf.

Pew Research Center. "Social Media Fact Sheet." February 05, 2018. Accessed September 1, 2018. http://www.pewinternet.org/fact-sheet/social-media/.

"Re:Work - Great Managers Still Matter: The Evolution of Google's Project Oxygen." Google. Accessed September 1, 2018. https://rework.withgoogle.com/blog/the-evolution-of-project-oxygen/.

Rosling, Sam. *Snoop: What Your Stuff Says About You.* New York, NY: Basic Books, 2008.

Schmidt, Tracy Samantha. "Inside the Backlash against Facebook." *Time* Magazine. September 6, 2006. http://www.time.com/time/nation/article/0,8599,1532225,00.html.

Stephens-Davidowitz, Seth. *Everybody Lies: Big Data, New Data, and What the Internet Reveals about Who We Really Are.* New York, NY: HarperCollins, 2017.

Shearer, Elisa, and Jeffrey Gottfried. "News Use Across Social Media Platforms 2017." Pew Research Center's Journalism Project. September 07, 2017. Accessed September 1, 2018. http://www.journalism.org/2017/09/07/news-use-across-social-media-platforms-2017/.

Walpole, Horace. *Letters Addressed to the Countess of Ossory: From the Year 1769 to 1797*, Volume 2. Edited by Vernon Smith. London: Richard Bentley, 1848.

Walpole, Horace. *The Letters of Horace Walpole, Earl of Orford.* Volume 2. 1749–1759. Project Gutenberg. Accessed September 1, 2018. https://www.gutenberg.org/ebooks/4610.

Wilson, Richard. *Croome Court, Worcestershire.* 1758–59 (undated). Private Collection, England.

Wilson, Richard. *An Extensive View of Croome Court, Worcestershire, from the South 1758.* Oil on canvas, 381 x 508 mm. Croome Park, Worcestershire. http://www.nationaltrustcollections.org.uk/object/170904.

THREE: YOU ARE THE EXPERT

Aquinas, Thomas. Trans. Fathers of the English Dominican Province. *Summa Theologica*, Part I (Prima Pars) From the Complete American Edition. Project

BIBLIOGRAPHY

Gutenberg. Accessed September 01, 2018. https://www.gutenberg.org/ebooks/17611.

Bornstein, David. "A Better Way to Teach Math." *The New York Times.* April 18, 2011. Accessed September 1, 2018. https://opinionator.blogs.nytimes.com/2011/04/18/a-better-way-to-teach-math/.

Buonarroti, Michael Angelo and Tommaso Campanella. *The Sonnets of Michael Angelo Buonarroti and Tommaso Campanella.* Translated by John Addington Symonds. 1878.

Burns, Robert. *The Complete Works of Robert Burns*: Containing His Poems, Songs, and Correspondence. Ed. Allan Cunningham. Boston: Phillips, Sampson, and Company, 1855.

Catmull, Ed and Amy Wallace. *Creativity, Inc.: Overcoming the Unseen Forces That Stand in the Way of True Inspiration.* Random House Publishing Group. Kindle.

Cialdini, Robert B. *Influence: The Psychology of Persuasion.* New York, NY: Collins, 2006.

Edgerton, Samuel Y., Jr. *The Renaissance Rediscovery of Linear Perspective.* New York, NY: Basic Books, 1975.

Iyengar, Sheena S., and Mark R. Lepper. "When choice is demotivating: Can one desire too much of a good thing?" *Journal of Personality and Social Psychology* 79, no. 6 (2000): 995–1006. http://dx.doi.org/10.1037/0022-3514.79.6.995.

Jefferson, Thomas. "To John Adams from Thomas Jefferson, 1 August 1816," Founders Online, National Archives, last modified June 13, 2018. http://founders.archives.gov/documents/Adams/99-02-02-6618.

Justus, Barry, Baldo Gucciardi, and Michael Flint. "Living on the Edge." *Pool & Spa Marketing* (October 2015): 18-26.

Justus, Barry. "Working on the Road." WaterShapes. Accessed September 1, 2018. https://watershapes.com/professional-watershaping/working-on-the-raod.html.

Klee, Paul. *Tribüne der Kunst und Zeit. Eine Schriftensammlung.* Herausgegeben von [Published by] Kasimir Edschmid. XIII. Schöpferische Konfession. Berlin. Erich Reiß Verlag. 1920.

Kreiser, John. "Slap Shot the Weapon of Hockey's Hardest Shooter." NHL.

com. August 26, 2012. https://www.nhl.com/news/slap-shot-the-weapon-of-hockeys-hardest-shooters/c-640429.

Norton, Michael I., Daniel Mochon, and Dan Ariely. "The IKEA Effect: When Labor Leads to Love." *Journal of Consumer Psychology* 22, Issue 3 (July 2012): 453–460. https://doi.org/10.1016/j.jcps.2011.08.002.

Oliva, Aude. "The Art of Hybrid Images: Two for the View of One." *Art & Perception* 1, no. 1-2 (2013): 65-74. https://doi.org/10.1163/22134913-00002004.

"Overview of U.S. Renovation in 2016 and 2017." Houzz. 2017. Accessed September 1, 2018. http://st.hzcdn.com/static/econ/HouzzAndHome2017.pdf.

"Re:work." Google. Accessed September 1, 2018. https://rework.withgoogle.com/print/guides/5721312655835136/.

Shaffer, D. M., A. B. Maynor, and W. L. Roy. "The Visual Perception of Lines on the Road." *Perception & Psychophysics* 70, no. 8 (2008): 1571-580. Accessed September 1, 2018. https://doi:10.3758/pp.70.8.1571.

Sterne, Laurence. *The Life and Opinions of Tristram Shandy, Gentleman*. 1759.

"Table DL-20 - Highway Statistics 2015 - Policy and Governmental Affairs. Federal Highway Administration." U.S. Department of Transportation/Federal Highway Administration. Accessed September 1, 2018. https://www.fhwa.dot.gov/policyinformation/statistics/2015/dl20.cfm.

US Department of Transportation. "3.2 Trillion Miles Driven On U.S. Roads In 2016." Accessed September 1, 2018. https://www.fhwa.dot.gov/pressroom/fhwa1704.cfm.

Vasari, Giorgio. *Lives of the Most Eminent Painters, Sculptors, & Architects.* Volume IX: Michelagnolo to the Flemings. Translated by Gaston Du C. De Vere. 1915.

Witt, Jessica K., and Dennis R. Proffitt. "See the Ball, Hit the Ball: Apparent Ball Size Is Correlated With Batting Average." *Psychological Science* 16, no. 12 (December 2005): 937–938. Accessed September 1, 2018. https://doi:10.1037/e537052012-029.

BIBLIOGRAPHY

FOUR: DESIGN IN 3D—AND IN PHASES

Barasz, Kate. "Research: If You Position Products as a Set, People Are More Likely to Buy Them All." *Harvard Business Review*. November 15, 2017. https://hbr.org/2017/11/research-if-you-position-products-as-a-set-people-are-more-likely-to-buy-them-all.

Barasz, K., John, L. K., Keenan, E. A., and Norton, M. I. "Pseudo-set Framing." *Journal of Experimental Psychology: General* 146, no. 10 (2017): 1460–1477. http://dx.doi.org/10.1037/xge0000337.

Burchard, Hank. "Models of the Renaissance." *The Washington Post*. December 23, 1994. https://www.washingtonpost.com/archive/lifestyle/1994/12/23/models-of-the-renaissance/65f68385-53cc-49b4-85da-b9bd014b4b15/.

Da Vinci, Leonardo. *Mona Lisa*. 1503–1506. Oil on wood. Louvre, Paris.

"Dove Vai?—New View of the Cricket Cage." *Tuscan Traveler*. November 10, 2008. http://tuscantraveler.com/2008/florence/new-view-dagnolo-duomo-brunelleschi-dome.

Harris, Beth and Steven Zucker. "Linear Perspective: Brunelleschi's Experiment" (video). Khan Academy. Accessed September 1, 2018. https://www.khanacademy.org/humanities/renaissance-reformation/early-renaissance1/beginners-renaissance-florence/v/linear-perspective-brunelleschi-s-experiement.

King, Ross. *Brunelleschi's Dome: How a Renaissance Genius Reinvented Architecture*. Bloomsbury Publishing, 2000. Kindle.

Picasso, Pablo. *Guernica*. Oil on canvas, 349.3 x 776.6 cm. https://www.museoreinasofia.es/en/collection/artwork/guernica.

Pogrebin, Robin, and Scott Reyburn. "Leonardo Da Vinci Painting Sells for $450.3 Million, Shattering Auction Highs." *The New York Times*. November 15, 2017. Accessed September 1, 2018. https://www.nytimes.com/2017/11/15/arts/design/leonardo-da-vinci-salvator-mundi-christies-auction.html.

Prager, Frank D., and Gustina Scaglia. *Brunelleschi: Studies of His Technology and Inventions*. Mineola, NY: Dover, 1970.

Thompson, Don. *The $12 Million Stuffed Shark: The Curious Economics of Contemporary Art*. New York: St. Martin's Press, 2008. Kindle.

Tuttle, Brad. "You Can Buy the Mona Lisa for $25,000." *Time*, October 2, 2014. Accessed September 1, 2018. http://time.com/money/3457030/mona-lisa-forgery-sale-mark-landis/.

Vasari, Giorgio. *Lives of the Most Eminent Painters Sculptors and Architects*. Vol. 4, Filippino Lippi to Domenico Puligo. Translated by Gaston du C. De Vere. 1913.

Filimon, Flavia. "Are All Spatial Reference Frames Egocentric? Reinterpreting Evidence for Allocentric, Object-Centered, or World-Centered Reference Frames." *Frontiers in Human Neuroscience* 9 (December 9, 2015): 648. https://doi.org/doi: 10.3389/fnhum.2015.00648. PMID: 26696861; PMCID: PMC4673307.

"When Picasso Put Down His Brushes and Painted With Light Instead - Google Arts & Culture." Google. Accessed October 1, 2018. https://artsandculture.google.com/theme/lgLSm8J028B8KQ.

FIVE: SURPRISE YOUR CLIENTS

Gawande, Atul. *The Checklist Manifesto: How to Get Things Right*. New York: Metropolitan Books, 2009.

Lowry, Brian. "'Seinfeld's' Finale Ends Up in Sixth Place of All Time." *Los Angeles Times*. May 16, 1998. https://www.latimes.com/archives/la-xpm-1998-may-16-ca-50143-story.html.

Maas, Jane. *Mad Women*. New York: St. Martin's Press, 2012. Kindle.

"The Motive Power of the Future: Mr Edison's Ideas." *The Bankers' Magazine of Australasia* 10, No. 1, From August 1896 to July 1897. Edited by Clement H. Davis. Melbourne: Robt. Lascelles & Co., August 1896.

Perloff, Richard M. *Dynamics of Persuasion: Communication and Attitudes in the 21st Century*. New York: Lawrence Erlbaum Associates, 2008.

"Why people need to 'know before they go.'" *Think with Google*. https://www.thinkwithgoogle.com/feature/search-insights/#/.

SIX: CREATE AN EXPERIENCE

The ALS Association. "ALS Ice Bucket Challenge Donations Lead to Significant Gene Discovery." News release. July 25, 2016. http://www.alsa.org/news/media/press-releases/significant-gene-discovery-072516.html.

The ALS Association. "ALS Ice Bucket Challenge - FAQ." http://www.alsa.org/about-us/ice-bucket-challenge-faq.html.

The ALS Association. "The Amyotrophic Lateral Sclerosis Association Financial Statements, January 31, 2015 and 2014." Long Beach, CA: May 10, 2015. http://www.alsa.org/assets/pdfs/fye15_fin_statement.pdf.

The ALS Association. "Every Drop Adds Up." http://www.alsa.org/fight-als/ice-bucket-challenge.html.

Berkman, Lisa F. and S. Leonard Syme. "Social Networks, Host Resistance, and Mortality: A Nine-Year Follow-Up Study of Alameda County Residents." *American Journal of Epidemiology* 109, Issue 2 (February 1979): 186–204. https://doi.org/10.1093/oxfordjournals.aje.a112674.

Boothby, Erica J. Boothby, Margaret S. Clark, and John A. Bargh, "Shared Experiences Are Amplified." *Psychological Science* 25, Issue 12 (2014). doi.org/10.1177/0956797614551162.

Carbon, Claus-Christian. "Understanding human perception by human-made illusions." *Frontiers in Human Neuroscience* 8, article 566 (July 2014). https://doi.org/10.3389/fnhum.2014.00566.

Drucker, Peter F. *The Essential Drucker*. New York: HarperCollins, 2001.

Gawdat, Mo. *Solve for Happy: Engineer Your Path to Joy*. New York: North Star Way, 2017.

House, James S., Cynthia Robbins, and Helen L. Metzner. "The Association of Social Relationships and Activities with Mortality: Prospective Evidence from the Tecumseh Community Health Study." *American Journal of Epidemiology* 16, Issue 1 (July 1982): 123–140. https://doi.org/10.1093/oxfordjournals.aje.a113387.

"Ice Cream and Frozen Custard." *Electronic Code of Federal Regulations*, Title 21: Food and Drugs, Part 135: Frozen Desserts, Subpart B: Requirements for

Specific Standardized Frozen Desserts (March 28, 2019). https://www.ecfr.gov.

Iyengar, Sheena. *The Art of Choosing*. New York: Twelve, 2010.

Jefferson, Thomas. Thomas Jefferson to John Adams. August 1, 1816. In *Papers of Thomas Jefferson: Retirement Series,* vol. 10, 1 May 1816 to 18 January 1817. Edited by J. Jefferson Looney. Princeton and Oxford: Princeton University Press, 2013.

Kotler, Philip, Neil Rackham, and Suj Krishnaswamy. "Ending the War Between Sales and Marketing." Harvard Business Review. July–August 2006. https://hbr.org/2006/07/ending-the-war-between-sales-and-marketing.

Kumar, Amit, Matthew A. Killingsworth, and Thomas Gilovich. "Waiting for Merlot: Anticipatory Consumption of Experiential and Material Purchases." *Psychological Science* 25, Issue 10 (2014). https://doi.org/10.1177/0956797614546556.

Levav, Jonathan, Mark Heitmann, Andreas Herrmann, and Sheena S. Iyengar. "Order in Product Customization Decisions: Evidence from Field Experiments." *Journal of Political Economy* 118, no. 2 (2010): 274–299.

O'Connor, Anahad. "The Secrets to a Happy Life, From a Harvard Study." *The New York Times*. March 23, 2016. https://well.blogs.nytimes.com/2016/03/23/the-secrets-to-a-happy-life-from-a-harvard-study.

Schwartz, Barry. *The Paradox of Choice: Why More Is Less*. New York: Ecco, 2004.

Shenhava, Amitai and Randy L. Bucknera. "Neural Correlates of Dueling Affective Reactions to Win–Win Choices." *PNAS* 111, no. 30 (July 29, 2014): 10978–10983.

Shimer, David. "Yale's Most Popular Class Ever: Happiness." *The New York Times*. January 26, 2018. https://www.nytimes.com/2018/01/26/nyregion/at-yale-class-on-happiness-draws-huge-crowd-laurie-santos.html.

Simon, Herbert. "Rational Choice and the Structure of the Environment." *Psychological Review* 63, no. 2 (1956): 129–138. http://dx.doi.org/10.1037/h0042769.

Smith, Kirsten P. and Nicholas A. Christakis. "Social Networks and Health."

Annual Review of Sociology, Vol. 34 (August 2008): 405–429. https://doi.org/10.1146/annurev.soc.34.040507.134601.

Sutherland, Rory. *Rory Sutherland: The Wiki Man*. It's Nice That and Ogilvy Digital Labs, 2011. Kindle.

Thaler, Richard H. and Cass R. Sunstein. *Nudge: Improving Decisions About Health, Wealth, and Happiness*. New York: Penguin, 2008.

Umberson, Debra, and Jennifer Karas Montez. "Social Relationships and Health: A Flashpoint for Health Policy." *Journal of Health and Social Behavior* 51, issue 1 (October 8, 2010): S54–S66. https://doi.org/10.1177/0022146510383501.

Zoltners, Andris A., PK Sinha, and Sally E. Lorimer. "Why Sales and Marketing Don't Get Along." *Harvard Business Review*. November 04, 2013. https://hbr.org/2013/11/why-sales-and-marketing-dont-get-along.

SEVEN: SHARE WITH PURPOSE

"A Chicago tale: Why we're happy to erase the asterisk from Daniel Burnham's 'Make no little plans.*'" *Chicago Tribune*. March 6, 2019. https://www.chicagotribune.com/opinion/editorials/ct-edit-daniel-burnham-quote-20190305-story.html.

Barker, Henry Aston. *A series of eight views forming a panorama of the celebrated city of Constantinople and its' environs, taken from the town of Galata, by Henry Aston Barker, and exhibited in his Great Rotunda, Leicester Square*. London: Thomas Palser, 1813.

"Be Transported." Museum of Science and Industry, updated February 29, 2016. https://www.msichicago.org/explore/whats-here/exhibits/great-train-story/.

Feiman, Jesse. "The Matrix and the Meaning in Dürer's Rhinoceros." *Art in Print* 2, no. 4 (2012): 22–26. http://www.jstor.org/stable/43047078.

Garcia-Fenech, Giovanni. "Dürer and the elusive rhino." The Artstor Blog. February 11, 2014. https://artstor.wordpress.com/2014/02/11/depicting-the-elusive-rhino/.

Herbal, c. 1440. Catalogue of Illuminated Manuscripts. British Library.

https://www.bl.uk/catalogues/illuminatedmanuscripts/record.asp?MSID=7796&CollID=9&NStart=4016.

Kesby, Rebecca. "How the world's first webcam made a coffee pot famous." BBC News, November 22, 2012. https://www.bbc.com/news/technology-20439301.

Lewis, Meriwether, and William Clark. *The Journals of Lewis and Clark*, 1804 1806.

"Melted Chocolate to Microwave: An imaginative engineer turned a mess into a universal machine." *Technology Review*. January 1, 1999. https://www.technologyreview.com/s/400335/melted-chocolate-to-microwave/.

"Mobile Fact Sheet." Pew Research Center. February 5, 2018. https://www.pewinternet.org/fact-sheet/mobile/.

Montgomery, Lucy Maud. *Anne of Green Gables*. 1908.

Mueller, Tom. "Mystery of Florence's Cathedral Dome May Be Solved." *National Geographic*. February 10, 2014. https://news.nationalgeographic.com/news/2014/02/140210-duomo-florence-brunelleschi-cathedral-architecture/.

Norman, Dan. *The Design of Everyday Things*. Revised and Expanded Edition. New York: Basic Books, 2013.

Talbot, William Henry Fox. *The Pencil of Nature*. London: Longman, Brown, Green and Longmans, 1844.

Vincent van Gogh to Theo van Gogh, Ramsgate, May 31, 1876.

Vuko, Evelyn Porreca. "Animal Encounters." *Smithsonian Education*. 2013. http://www.smithsonianeducation.org/educators/lesson_plans/lewis_clark/lesson1_main.html.

APPENDIX: HOW TO CHARGE FOR YOUR DESIGNS

Buonarroti, Michael Angelo and Tommaso Campanella. *The Sonnets of Michael Angelo Buonarroti and Tommaso Campanella*. Translated by John Addington Symonds. 1878.

BIBLIOGRAPHY

Khan, Gulnaz. "This Temple Honors the Egyptian Queen Who Ruled As King." *National Geographic.* https://www.nationalgeographic.com/travel/destinations/africa/egypt/luxor-temple-of-hatshepsut-theban-necropolis/.

Sutherland, Ivan. "The Ultimate Display." *Proceedings of IFIP* 65, vol 2 (1965): 506–508.

ABOUT THE AUTHOR

Noah Nehlich is the founder of Structure Studios. For the past two decades, Noah has helped thousands of designers, builders, and salespeople leverage 3D design tools to amaze their clients and achieve their business goals.

Ever since he skipped college in favor of developing 3D outdoor living design software, Noah has recognized that great designs offer far more than concrete and water. The most compelling designs are the ones that create an emotional connection. That's why his goal is to improve lives through 3D experiences.

As an entrepreneur, investor, and tech company enthusiast, Noah's into everything 3D. He lives in Henderson, Nevada with his wife, Stefanie; son, Wesley; daughter, Whitney; and dog, Riley.

Made in the USA
Monee, IL
04 January 2022